Collins easy learning

My first dictionary

Ages 4–5

asleep *adjective*

crab *noun*

sing *verb*

How to use this book

- Find a quiet, comfortable place to look at this book, away from distractions.

- Read the words, meanings and examples with your child, letting them talk about the pictures and look at the words and letters.

- This book gives your child an easy and fun introduction to using a dictionary. Working with this book, you and your child can enjoy looking up the meanings of words together, using the many examples and illustrations to help you.

- Always end your session before your child gets tired so they will be eager to return next time.

- Give your child plenty of praise and encouragement as you work together with this book.

- Let your child return to their favourite words, pictures and pages and talk about what they like and what they have learnt.

Special features of this book:

- The words included in this dictionary have been carefully selected to include many nouns, adjectives and verbs with which your child will already be familiar. Discuss with your child what they think the word means and how they would use it. Engaging your child in a discussion about language will help to stimulate their interest and develop an early love of learning.

- The initial sound of every word has been highlighted in a different colour to encourage children to identify the individual letter sounds and shapes. Help your child to practise these sounds and find other words in the dictionary which contain the same sound.

- Many children enjoy using rhyme at an early age. Simple words which have a common rhyming pattern, for example, *bin*, *cat*, *tap* have been shown throughout this dictionary. Read them with your child, emphasizing the rhyming sound and encouraging them to use rhyme for themselves.

- Look out for the *Tip* boxes which tell you about compound words, two words which are joined together to make a new word. Help your child think of other similar words, or ask them to invent some of their own!

HarperCollins Publishers
Westerhill Road
Bishopbriggs
Glasgow
G64 2QT

First Edition 2016
10 9 8 7 6 5 4 3 2 1

© HarperCollins Publishers 2016

ISBN 978-0-00-820948-3

www.collins.co.uk

Printed and bound in China by
RR Donnelley APS Co. Ltd

A catalogue record for this book is available from the British Library.

MANAGING EDITOR
Maree Airlie

FOR THE PUBLISHER
Gerry Breslin
Sarah Woods

CONTRIBUTORS
Carol Medcalf
Carole Asquith
Jenny Tulip

ILLUSTRATIONS
© HarperCollins Publishers

Contents

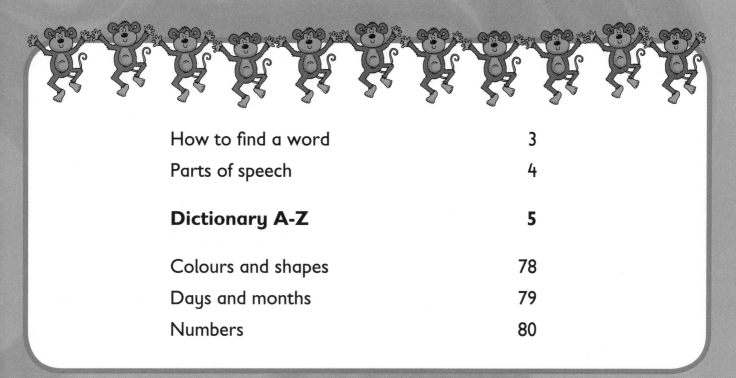

How to find a word

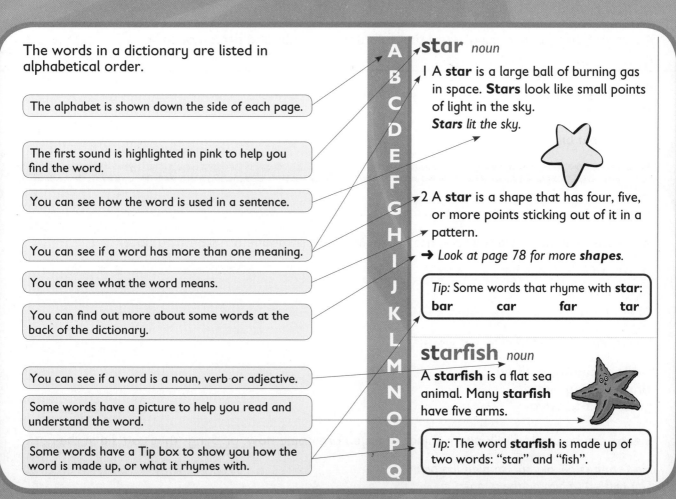

The words in a dictionary are listed in alphabetical order.

The alphabet is shown down the side of each page.

The first sound is highlighted in pink to help you find the word.

You can see how the word is used in a sentence.

You can see if a word has more than one meaning.

You can see what the word means.

You can find out more about some words at the back of the dictionary.

You can see if a word is a noun, verb or adjective.

Some words have a picture to help you read and understand the word.

Some words have a Tip box to show you how the word is made up, or what it rhymes with.

star *noun*

1 A **star** is a large ball of burning gas in space. **Stars** look like small points of light in the sky. *Stars lit the sky.*

2 A **star** is a shape that has four, five, or more points sticking out of it in a pattern.

→ *Look at page 78 for more* **shapes**.

Tip: Some words that rhyme with **star**:
bar   car   far   tar

starfish *noun*

A **starfish** is a flat sea animal. Many **starfish** have five arms.

Tip: The word **starfish** is made up of two words: "star" and "fish".

Parts of speech

Nouns

A **noun** is a 'naming' word that is used for talking about a person or thing.

arm *noun*
bird *noun*
computer *noun*

*We played games on our **computer**.*

If you are talking about more than one of the thing, you usually add **s** to the end of the word.

*She stretched her **arms** out.*

Proper nouns are the names of people, places, days and months, and <u>always</u> start with a capital letter.

June *noun*
Monday *noun*

*She started school on **Monday**.*

Adjectives

An **adjective** is a 'describing' word that tells you more about a person or thing.

big *adjective*
happy *adjective*
wet *adjective*

*She lives in a **big** house.*

Verbs

A **verb** is a 'doing' word that you use for saying what someone or something does.

walk *verb*
sing *verb*
give *verb*

Verbs can be used in different ways.

walk, walking, walked
sing, singing, sang
give, giving, gave

Verbs can be used to talk about things that you are doing now, or things that you did in the past.

*He **teaches** people how to play the piano.*
*She **talked** to him on the phone.*

Aa

aeroplane *noun*

An **aeroplane** is a large vehicle with wings and engines that flies through the air.

afternoon *noun*

The **afternoon** is the part of each day between twelve noon and about six o'clock.

> *Tip:* The word **afternoon** is made up of two words: "after" and "noon".

age *noun*

Your **age** is the number of years that you have lived.
*What **age** are you?*

> *Tip:* Some words that rhyme with **age:**
> cage   page   rage   stage

air *noun*

Air is the mixture of gases all around us that we breathe.
*I opened the window to let in some **air**.*

> *Tip:* Some words that rhyme with **air:**
> chair   fair   hair   pair

airport *noun*

An **airport** is a place where aeroplanes take off and land.

> *Tip:* The word **airport** is made up of two words: "air" and "port".

alarm *noun*

An **alarm** is a piece of equipment that warns you of danger by making a noise.
*The car **alarm** woke us up.*

alien *noun*

In stories and films, an **alien** is a creature from another planet.

all

You use **all** to talk about everything, everyone, or the whole of something.
*Will the caterpillar eat **all** of the apple?*

> *Tip:* Some words that rhyme with **all:**
> ball   call   fall   tall   wall

alligator *noun*

An **alligator** is a large reptile with a long body, a long mouth and sharp teeth. **Alligators'** mouths are in the shape of a letter U.

a b c d e f g h i j k l m n o p q r s t u v w x y z

alphabet *noun*

An **alphabet** is a set of letters that is used for writing words. The letters are arranged in a special order.
"a" is the first letter of the **alphabet**.

Tip: The word **alphabet** is made up of the first two letters of the Greek alphabet.

always

If you **always** do something, you do it every time or all the time.
*She is **always** late for school.*

ambulance *noun*

An **ambulance** is a vehicle for taking people to hospital.

angry *adjective*

When you are **angry**, you feel very upset about something.
*He was **angry** at his brother for breaking the window.*

animal *noun*

An **animal** is any creature that is alive, but not a plant or a person.
*What kind of **animal** is that?*

ankle *noun*

Your **ankle** is the part of your body where your foot joins your leg.
*I fell and twisted my **ankle**.*

ant *noun*

Ants are small insects that live in large groups.

apple *noun*

An **apple** is a firm, round fruit with green, red, or yellow skin.

apron *noun*

An **apron** is a large piece of cloth that you wear over your other clothes to keep them clean when you are doing something like cooking or painting.

arm *noun*

Your **arms** are the two parts of your body between your shoulders and your hands.
*She stretched her **arms** out.*

arrow *noun*

An **arrow** is a sign that shows you which way to go.
*Follow the **arrows** along the path.*

art *noun*

Art is drawing or painting, or something that someone has drawn or painted.

Tip: Some words that rhyme with **art**:
chart **dart** **part** **start**

ask *verb*

1 If you **ask** someone a question, you say that you want to know something.
*Shall I **ask** him what his name is?*

2 If you **ask** for something, you say that you want it.
*She was too shy to **ask** for any sweets.*

asleep *adjective*

If you are **asleep**, you are sleeping.
*The cat was fast **asleep**.*

assembly *noun*

An **assembly** is a group of people who meet together.
*We were late for school **assembly**.*

astronaut *noun*

An **astronaut** is a person who travels in space.
*When I grow up I want to be an **astronaut**.*

aunt *noun*

Your **aunt** is the sister of your mother or father, or the wife of their brother or sister.

awake *adjective*

Someone who is **awake** is not sleeping.
*I was **awake** early this morning.*

away

If you put something **away**, you put it where it should be.
*Put your books **away** before you go.*

Tip: Some words that rhyme with **away**:
day **may** **play** **say** **way**

awful *adjective*

If something is **awful**, it is very bad.
*There was an **awful** smell coming from the bin.*

a b c d e f g h i j k l m n o p q r s t u v w x y z

Bb

baby *noun*

A **baby** is a very young child.

back *noun*

Your **back** is the part of your body from your neck to your bottom.
*He was lying on his **back** in the grass.*

> *Tip:* Some words that rhyme with **back:**
> **black   pack   quack   sack   track**

bad *adjective*

Someone who is **bad** does things they should not do.
*A **bad** man stole the money.*

> *Tip:* Some words that rhyme with **bad:**
> **dad   had   mad   pad   sad**

bag *noun*

A **bag** is a container that you use to hold or carry things.
*He put his shoes in his **bag**.*

ball *noun*

A **ball** is a round thing that you kick, throw or catch in games.

> *Tip:* Some words that rhyme with **ball:**
> **all   call   fall   tall   wall**

balloon *noun*

A **balloon** is a small bag made of thin rubber that you blow into to make it bigger.

banana *noun*

A **banana** is a long curved fruit with a thick, yellow skin.

bang *noun*

A **bang** is a sudden, loud noise.
*The balloon burst with a **bang**.*

bark *verb*

When a dog **barks**, it makes a short, loud noise.

bat *noun*

1 A **bat** is a special stick that you use to hit a ball in some games.
2 A **bat** is also a small animal like a mouse with wings that flies at night.

> *Tip:* Some words that rhyme with **bat:**
> **cat   fat   hat   mat   rat**

A B C D E F G H I J K L M N O P Q R S T U V W X Y Z

bath *noun*

A **bath** is a long container that you fill with water and sit in to wash yourself.

bathroom *noun*

A **bathroom** is a room with a bath or shower in it.

> *Tip:* The word **bathroom** is made up of two words: "bath" and "room".

beach *noun*

A **beach** is the land by the edge of the sea. It is covered with sand or stones.

bear *noun*

A **bear** is a big, strong animal with thick fur and sharp claws.

bed *noun*

A **bed** is a piece of furniture that you lie on when you sleep.

bedroom *noun*

A **bedroom** is a room with a bed in it where you sleep.

> *Tip:* The word **bedroom** is made up of two words: "bed" and "room".

bee *noun*

A **bee** is an insect with wings and black and yellow stripes on its body. **Bees** live in large groups and make honey.

> *Tip:* Some words that rhyme with **bee:**
> free   knee   see   three   tree

beetle *noun*

A **beetle** is an insect with wings that cover its body when it is not flying.

bell *noun*

A **bell** is a piece of metal in the shape of a cup that rings when you shake it or when something hits it.
*School starts when the **bell** rings.*

> *Tip:* Some words that rhyme with **bell:**
> fell   sell   shell   tell   well

belt *noun*

A **belt** is a band of leather or cloth that you wear around your waist.

best

If you say that something is **best**, you mean that it is better than all the others.
*You are my **best** friend.*

> *Tip:* Some words that rhyme with **best:**
> nest   test   vest   west

a b c d e f g h i j k l m n o p q r s t u v w x y z

bicycle *noun*

A **bicycle** is a vehicle with two wheels. You push the pedals with your feet to make the wheels turn.

big *adjective*

A person or thing that is **big** is large in size.
*She lives in a **big** house.*

> *Tip:* Some words that rhyme with **big**:
> **dig   pig   tig   twig   wig**

bike *noun*

A **bike** is a bicycle or motorbike.

bin *noun*

A **bin** is a container that you put rubbish in.

> *Tip:* Some words that rhyme with **bin**:
> **chin   pin   tin   twin   win**

bird *noun*

A **bird** is an animal with feathers, wings, and a beak. Most **birds** can fly.

black *noun*

Black is the colour of the sky at night.
*The car is **black**.*

> *Tip:* Some words that rhyme with **black**:
> **back   pack   quack   sack   track**

→ *Look at page 78 for more **colours**.*

blue *noun*

Blue is the colour of the sky on a sunny day.
*Her dress is **blue**.*

→ *Look at page 78 for more **colours**.*

boat *noun*

A **boat** is a small vehicle that carries people on water.

> *Tip:* Some words that rhyme with **boat**:
> **coat   float   goat   moat   stoat**

body *noun*

A person's or animal's **body** is all their parts.
*It's fun to stretch and twist your **body**.*

book *noun*

A **book** is a set of pages with words or pictures on them, that are held together inside a cover.

> *Tip:* Some words that rhyme with **book**:
> **cook   hook   look   shook   took**

boot *noun*

A **boot** is a kind of shoe that covers your foot and the lower part of your leg.

bottle *noun*

A **bottle** is a container made of glass or plastic that holds liquid.

box *noun*

A **box** is a container with a hard, straight bottom and sides, and usually a lid.

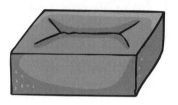

boy *noun*

A **boy** is a male child.

bread *noun*

Bread is a food that is made from flour and water and baked in an oven.

breakfast *noun*

Breakfast is the first meal of the day.

Tip: The word **breakfast** is made up of two words: "break" and "fast".

bridge *noun*

A **bridge** is something that is built over a river, a road, or a railway so that people can get across it.

bring *verb*

If you **bring** something, you take it with you when you go somewhere.
*You can **bring** a friend to the party.*

Tip: Some words that rhyme with **bring**:
king   sing   sting   thing   wing

brother *noun*

Your **brother** is a boy or a man who has the same mother and father as you do.

brown *noun*

Brown is the colour of earth or wood.
*Her eyes are dark **brown**.*

Tip: Some words that rhyme with **brown**:
clown   crown   down   frown   town

➔ *Look at page 78 for more **colours**.*

brush *noun*

A **brush** has lots of short hairs fixed to a handle. You use different types of **brushes** to make your hair tidy, to clean things, or to paint.
*There is too much paint on my **brush**.*

a b c d e f g h i j k l m n o p q r s t u v w x y z

bucket *noun*

A **bucket** is a deep, round container with a handle that you use to hold or carry liquids.

budgie *noun*

Budgies are small brightly-coloured birds, often kept as pets.

bug *noun*

A **bug** is a small insect.

Tip: Some words that rhyme with **bug**:
hug   jug   mug   rug   slug

bull *noun*

A **bull** is a male cow. **Bulls** have horns.

burn *verb*

If you **burn** yourself, you touch something that is hot and get hurt.
*I didn't want to **burn** myself on the hot iron.*

bus *noun*

A **bus** is a large vehicle that carries lots of people.
*I go to school on the **bus**.*

butter *noun*

Butter is a soft yellow food that is made from cream. You spread it on bread or cook with it.

butterfly *noun*

A **butterfly** is an insect with four large wings.

Tip: The word **butterfly** is made up of two words: "butter" and "fly".

button *noun*

Buttons are small, round things on clothes that you push through holes to fasten the clothes together.

buy *verb*

If you **buy** something, you pay money so that you can have it.
*We went into the shop to **buy** a magazine.*

buzz *verb*

If something **buzzes**, it makes a rhyme with a bee makes when it flies.
*An insect started to **buzz** around my head.*

Cc

cage *noun*

A **cage** is a container or a room made of bars where you keep birds or animals.
*The bird had escaped from its **cage**.*

Tip: Some words that rhyme with **cage**:
age   page   rage   stage

cake *noun*

A **cake** is a sweet food made from flour, eggs, sugar, and butter which you bake in an oven.

Tip: Some words that rhyme with **cake**:
bake   lake   make   snake   take

calculator *noun*

A **calculator** is a small machine that you use to do sums.
*We are learning how to use a **calculator** at school.*

calf *noun*

A **calf** is a young cow.

call *verb*

If you **call** someone something, you give them a name.
*I decided to **call** my cat Pippin.*

Tip: Some words that rhyme with **call**:
all   ball   fall   tall   wall

camel *noun*

A **camel** is a large animal with one or two big lumps on its back. **Camels** live in hot, dry places and carry people and things.

camera *noun*

A **camera** is a machine that you use to take pictures.

can *verb*

If you **can** do something, you are able to do it.
*I **can** swim.*

Tip: Some words that rhyme with **can**:
fan   man   pan   ran   van

candle *noun*

A **candle** is a stick of wax with a piece of string through the middle that you burn to give you light.

car noun

A **car** is a vehicle with four wheels and an engine that can carry a small number of people.

Tip: Some words that rhyme with **car**:

| **bar** | **far** | **star** | **tar** |

caravan noun

A **caravan** is a vehicle pulled by a car in which people spend their holidays.

card noun

1 **Card** is stiff paper.

2 A **card** is a folded piece of stiff paper that has a picture on the front and a message inside. You send **cards** to people at special times, like birthdays.

3 **Cards** are pieces of stiff paper with numbers or pictures on them that you use for playing games.

carpet noun

A **carpet** is a thick, soft cover for a floor.
*My bedroom **carpet** is pink.*

carrot noun

A **carrot** is a long, orange vegetable.

cartoon noun

A **cartoon** is a film that uses drawings, not real people or things.
*I like to watch **cartoons** on Saturday morning.*

case noun

A **case** is a container that is used to hold or carry something.
*I took two **cases** on holiday.*

castle noun

A **castle** is a large building with very thick, high walls. Most **castles** were built a long time ago.

cat noun

A **cat** is an animal that is covered with fur and has a long tail. People often keep small **cats** as pets. Large **cats**, for example lions and tigers, are wild.

Tip: Some words that rhyme with **cat**:

| **bat** | **fat** | **hat** | **mat** | **rat** |

catch *verb*

If you **catch** something that is moving, you take hold of it while it is in the air.
*I tried to **catch** the ball.*

caterpillar *noun*

A **caterpillar** is a small animal that looks like a worm with lots of short legs. **Caterpillars** turn into butterflies or moths.

CD *noun*

A **CD** is a round, flat piece of plastic that has music or information on it. **CD** is short for "compact disc".
*I put all the photos on a **CD**.*

cereal *noun*

Cereal is a food made from grains that you eat with milk for breakfast.

chair *noun*

A **chair** is a seat with a back and four legs, for one person.
*He suddenly got up from his **chair**.*

Tip: Some words that rhyme with **chair:**
air   fair   hair   pair

chalk *noun*

Chalk is a kind of soft rock. You use small sticks of **chalk** to write or draw on a blackboard.

cheek *noun*

Your **cheeks** are the sides of your face below your eyes.
*My **cheeks** were red.*

cheese *noun*

Cheese is a solid food that is made from milk.

cherry *noun*

A **cherry** is a small, round fruit with a hard stone in the middle. **Cherries** are red, black, or yellow.

chest *noun*

A **chest** is a large, heavy box, usually made of wood.
*The **chest** was full of golden treasure.*

chick *noun*

A **chick** is a very young bird.
*The **chicks** hatched this morning.*

Tip: Some words that rhyme with **chick:**
lick   pick   quick   stick   trick

a b c d e f g h i j k l m n o p q r s t u v w x y z

chicken *noun*

1 A **chicken** is a bird that is kept on a farm for its eggs and meat.

2 **Chicken** is also the meat that comes from chickens.

child *noun*

A **child** is a young boy or girl.

chin *noun*

Your **chin** is the part of your face below your mouth.

Tip: Some words that rhyme with chin:
bin   pin   tin   twin   win

chip *noun*

Chips or **potato chips** are thin pieces of potato fried in hot oil.

Tip: Some words that rhyme with **chip**:
lip   nip   ship   skip   zip

chocolate *noun*

Chocolate is a sweet brown food that is used to make sweets, cakes, and drinks.

cinema *noun*

A **cinema** is a place where people watch films.

circle *noun*

A **circle** is a round shape.

→ *Look at page 78 for more **shapes**.*

circus *noun*

A **circus** is a big tent where you go to see clowns and animals.

city *noun*

A **city** is a very big town where a lot of people live and work.

clap *verb*

When you **clap**, you hit your hands together to make a loud noise. People **clap** to show that they like something. *Everyone started to **clap** at the end of her song.*

class *noun*

A **class** is a group of people who are taught together.
*He is in my **class** at school.*

Tip: Some words that rhyme with class:
brass   glass   grass   pass

classroom noun

A **classroom** is a room in a school where children have lessons.

> *Tip:* The word **classroom** is made up of two words: "class" and "room".

claw noun

A bird's or an animal's **claws** are the hard, sharp, curved parts at the end of its feet.

clean adjective

Something that is **clean** does not have any dirt or marks on it.
Make sure your hands are clean.

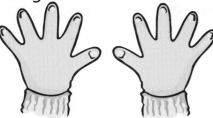

clever adjective

Someone who is **clever** can learn and understand things quickly.
She is very clever at maths.

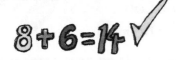

climb verb

If you **climb** something, you move towards the top of it. You sometimes use your hands as well as your feet when you **climb**.

> *Tip:* You do not say the "b" in the word **climb**. It sounds like **time**.

climbing frame noun

A **climbing frame** is a piece of playground equipment for climbing on.

> *Tip:* You do not say the "b" in the word **climbing**. It sounds like **timing**.

clip noun

A **clip** is something small and springy which holds things in place.
She took the clip out of her hair.

clock noun

A **clock** is a machine that shows you the time.

> *Tip:* Some words that rhyme with **clock**:
> **block   lock   rock   shock   sock**

close verb

When you **close** something, you shut it.
Please close the door behind you.

> *Tip:* When **close** means the same as "shut", it sounds like **nose**.

cloth noun

A **cloth** is a piece of material that you use to clean something.

clothes noun

Clothes are the things that people wear, for example shirts, trousers, and dresses.

cloud *noun*

A **cloud** is a white or grey shape that you see in the sky. **Clouds** are made up of tiny drops of water.

clown *noun*

A **clown** is a person who wears funny clothes and does silly things to make people laugh.

Tip: Some words that rhyme with **clown**: **brown crown down frown town**

coat *noun*

You wear a **coat** on top of your other clothes when you go outside.

Tip: Some words that rhyme with **coat**: **boat float goat moat stoat**

coffee *noun*

Coffee is a drink. You make it by pouring hot water on **coffee** beans.
Coffee beans grow on a coffee plant.

coin *noun*

A **coin** is a round, flat piece of metal that is used as money.

cold *adjective*

1 If you are **cold**, you do not feel comfortable because you are not warm enough.
Wear a jumper if you are cold.

2 If something is **cold**, it is not hot.
The weather is very cold.

colour *noun*

Red, blue and yellow are the main **colours**. You can mix them together to make other **colours**.

→ *Look at page 78 for some colours.*

comb *noun*

A **comb** is a flat piece of metal or plastic with very thin points that you use to make your hair tidy.

Tip: You do not say the "b" in the word **comb**. It sounds like **home**.

come *verb*

When you **come** to a place, you move towards it or arrive there.
"Come in!" he shouted.

comic _noun_

A **comic** is a magazine with stories that are told in pictures.

computer _noun_

A **computer** is a machine which can store a lot of information and can work things out very quickly.
We played games on our **computer**.

cone _noun_

A **cone** is the biscuit holder in which ice cream is served.
I had a **cone** with raspberry sauce.

cook _verb_

When you **cook** food, you make it hot and get it ready to eat.
Mum asked Dad to **cook** dinner.

> _Tip:_ Some words that rhyme with **cook**:
> **book**   **hook**   **look**   **shook**   **took**

cooker _noun_

A **cooker** is a machine that you use to cook food.

cool _adjective_

Someone or something that is **cool** is very good.
My new bike is so **cool**.

> _Tip:_ Some words that rhyme with **cool**:
> **fool**   **pool**   **stool**   **tool**

cot _noun_

A **cot** is a bed for a baby, with high sides to stop the baby from falling out.

> _Tip:_ Some words that rhyme with **cot**:
> **got**   **hot**   **not**   **pot**   **spot**

cotton wool _noun_

Cotton wool is soft fluffy cloth, often used for cleaning your skin.

count _verb_

When you **count**, you say numbers in order, one after the other.
I can **count** in French.

1 2 3
4 5 6
7 8 9

cousin _noun_

Your **cousin** is the son or daughter of your uncle or aunt.

cow _noun_

A **cow** is a large animal that is kept on farms because it gives milk.

> _Tip:_ Some words that rhyme with **cow**:
> **bow**   **how**   **now**   **wow**

crab _noun_

A **crab** is an animal with a hard shell that lives in the sea. **Crabs** have large pincers to catch their food.

crane *noun*

A **crane** is a tall machine that can lift very heavy things.

crash *noun*

1 A **crash** is an accident when a vehicle hits something.
*There was a car **crash** outside the school.*

2 A **crash** is also a sudden, loud noise.
*He dropped the plates with a **crash**.*

crawl *verb*

When you **crawl**, you move along on your hands and knees.
*The twins **crawl** along the floor.*

crayon *noun*

Crayons are sticks of wax in different colours that you use for drawing.

cricket *noun*

1 **Cricket** is a game where two teams take turns to hit a ball with a bat and run up and down.

2 A **cricket** is also a small jumping insect that rubs its wings together to make a high sound.

crisps *noun*

Crisps are thin pieces of fried potato that are eaten cold as a snack.
*May I have a packet of **crisps**?*

crocodile *noun*

A **crocodile** is a large reptile with a long body, a long mouth and sharp teeth. **Crocodiles'** mouths are in the shape of a letter V.

cross *noun*

A **cross** is a mark that you write. It looks like **X** or **+**.
*She put a **cross** beside my name.*

cross *adjective*

If you are **cross**, you feel angry about something.
*Mum was **cross** because we were late.*

crow *noun*

A **crow** is a large black bird.

crown *noun*

A **crown** is a circle made of gold or silver and jewels that kings and queens wear on their heads.

Tip: Some words that rhyme with **crown**:
brown   clown   down   frown   town

cry verb

When you **cry**, tears come from your eyes. People **cry** when they are sad or hurt.
The baby started to **cry**.

> *Tip:* Some words that rhyme with **cry**:
> **by   dry   fly   my   sky   try   why**

cub noun

A **cub** is a young wild animal, for example a young bear or lion.

cucumber noun

A **cucumber** is a long, thin, green vegetable that you eat in salads.

cup noun

A **cup** is a small, round container with a handle. You drink things like tea and coffee from a **cup**.
Would you like a **cup** *of tea?*

cupboard noun

A **cupboard** is a piece of furniture with a door and shelves that you keep things in.
The **cupboard** *was full of toys.*

> *Tip:* The word **cupboard** is made up of two words: "cup" and "board".

curly adjective

Curly hair is hair that has curved shapes in it.
She has long **curly** *hair.*

curtain noun

A **curtain** is a piece of cloth that you pull across a window to cover it.

cushion noun

A **cushion** is a bag of soft material that you put on a seat to make it more comfortable.

cut verb

If you **cut** something, you use a knife or scissors to divide it into pieces.
We **cut** *the cake.*

> *Tip:* Some words that rhyme with **cut**:
> **but   hut   nut   shut**

cut noun

A **cut** is a place on your skin where something sharp has gone through it.
He had a **cut** *on his finger.*

Dd

daffodil *noun*

A **daffodil** is a yellow flower that is shaped like a trumpet. **Daffodils** come out in spring.

daisy *noun*

A **daisy** is a small wild flower with white petals and a small yellow centre.

dance *verb*

When you **dance**, you move your body to music.

dark *adjective*

When it is **dark**, there is no light or not much light.

date *noun*

A **date** is the day, the month, or the year when something happens.
*What **date** is your birthday?*

day *noun*

1 A **day** is the length of time between one midnight and the next. There are twenty-four hours in a **day**, and seven **days** in a week.
*It is three **days** until my birthday.*

2 **Day** is the time when there is light outside.
*I've been busy all **day**.*

> Tip: Some words that rhyme with **day**:
> **away   may   play   say   way**

➔ *Look at page 79 for more about **days and months**.*

dead *adjective*

A person, an animal, or a plant that is **dead** has stopped living.

deep *adjective*

If something is **deep**, it goes down a long way.
*We dug a **deep** hole in the sand.*

deer *noun*

A **deer** is a large animal that lives in forests and can run very fast. Male **deer** have big horns that look like branches on their heads.

dentist *noun*

A **dentist** is a person whose job is to take care of people's teeth.
*I'm going to the **dentist** on Friday.*

desk *noun*

A **desk** is a kind of table that you sit at to write or to work.

*I sat at my **desk** to do my homework.*

diamond *noun*

A **diamond** is a shape with four straight sides.

➜ *Look at page 78 for more **shapes**.*

dice *noun*

A **dice** is a small cube with a different number of spots on each side. You throw **dice** in some games.

> *Tip:* Some words that rhyme with **dice**:
> **ice   mice   nice   rice   twice**

dig *verb*

If you **dig**, you make a hole in the ground.

*We need to **dig** a hole to plant the tree.*

> *Tip:* Some words that rhyme with **dig**:
> **big   pig   tig   twig   wig**

digger *noun*

A **digger** is a machine that is used for digging.

dinner *noun*

Dinner is the main meal of the day.
*What are we having for **dinner** today?*

dinosaur *noun*

Dinosaurs were animals that lived a very long time ago. Many **dinosaurs** were like very big lizards.

dirty *adjective*

If something is **dirty**, it has mud, food, or other marks on it.
*The dishes were **dirty**.*

dish *noun*

A **dish** is a container that you use to cook or serve food in.

do *verb*

If you **do** something, you spend some time on it or finish it.
*I tried to **do** some work.*

doctor *noun*

A **doctor** is a person whose job is to help people who are ill or hurt to get better.

dog *noun*

A **dog** is an animal that barks. Some **dogs** do special jobs, like helping blind people.

> *Tip:* Some words that rhyme with **dog**:
> **bog   fog   frog   log**

doll *noun*

A **doll** is a toy that looks like a small person or a baby.

dolphin *noun*

A **dolphin** is an animal that lives in the sea and looks like a large fish with a long nose. **Dolphins** are very clever.

donkey *noun*

A **donkey** is an animal that looks like a small horse with long ears.
*The farmer keeps a **donkey** in the field.*

door *noun*

You open and close a **door** to get into a building, a room, or a cupboard.
*The old man knocked three times on the **door**.*

down

When something moves **down**, it goes from a higher place to a lower place.
*She came **down** the stairs.*

> *Tip:* Some words that rhyme with **down**: **brown clown crown frown town**

dragon *noun*

In stories, a **dragon** is a monster that has wings and can make fire come out of its mouth.

dragonfly *noun*

A **dragonfly** is a small colourful insect with large wings which is often found near water.

> *Tip:* The word **dragonfly** is made up of two words: "dragon" and "fly".

draw *verb*

When you **draw**, you use pens, pencils, or crayons to make a picture.
*He likes to **draw** animals.*

dream *noun*

A **dream** is something you see and hear in your mind while you are sleeping.
*I had a **dream** about winning the prize.*

dress *noun*

A **dress** is something that you can wear. It covers the body and part of the legs.
*She wore a pink **dress**.*

drink verb

When you **drink**, you swallow liquid.
*My parents **drink** a lot of coffee.*

> *Tip:* Some words that rhyme with **drink**:
> **ink   pink   sink   think   wink**

drink noun

A **drink** is a liquid which you swallow
to stop you being thirsty.
*Please can I have a **drink**?*

drip verb

When liquid **drips**, a small amount of
it falls from somewhere.
*Water started to **drip** from the roof.*

> *Tip:* Some words that rhyme with **drip**:
> **chip   nip   ship   skip   zip**

drive verb

When someone **drives** a vehicle, they
make it go where they want.
*He has to **drive** for work.*

drum noun

A **drum** is an instrument which you hit
with sticks or with your hands to make
music.

dry adjective

If something is **dry**, there is no water
in it or on it.
*My clothes are **dry**.*

> *Tip:* Some words that rhyme with **dry**:
> **by   cry   fly   my   sky   try   why**

duck noun

A **duck** is a bird that lives near water
and can swim. **Ducks** have large flat
beaks.

> *Tip:* Some words that rhyme with **duck**:
> **luck   muck   stuck   suck   truck**

dust noun

Dust is tiny pieces of dry dirt that
looks like powder.
*The table was covered in **dust**.*

DVD noun

A **DVD** is a disc on which films or
music are recorded.

a b c **d** e f g h i j k l m n o p q r s t u v w x y z

Ee

ear noun

Your **ears** are the two parts of your body that you hear sounds with.
*He whispered something in her **ear**.*

Tip: Some words that rhyme with **ear**:
fear   gear   hear   near   year

early adjective

If you are **early**, you arrive before the time that you were expected to come.
*She was too **early** for the party.*

earth noun

The **Earth** is the planet that we live on.

easy adjective

If something is **easy**, you can do it or understand it without having to try very much.
*This sum is **easy**.*

eat verb

When you **eat**, you chew and swallow food.
*The children are going to **eat** their lunch.*

Tip: Some words that rhyme with **eat**:
heat   meat   neat   seat   treat

egg noun

Baby birds, insects, and some other animals grow in **eggs** until they are big enough to come out and be born. People often eat hens' **eggs** as food.

elbow noun

Your **elbow** is the part in the middle of your arm where it bends.
*She put her **elbows** on the table.*

elephant noun

An **elephant** is a very large, grey animal with big ears and a long nose called a trunk. Some **elephants** have two long, curved teeth called tusks.

email *noun*

An **email** is a message like a letter that you send from one computer or phone to another.
*I got an **email** from my cousin.*

empty *adjective*

If something is **empty**, there is nothing inside it.
*The glass was **empty**.*

end *noun*

The **end** of something is the last part of it.
*He told me the **end** of the story.*

Tip: Some words that rhyme with **end**:
bend   lend   mend   send   spend

enormous *adjective*

Something that is **enormous** is very big.
*The giant is **enormous**.*

envelope *noun*

An **envelope** is a paper cover that you put a letter or a card into before you send it to someone.

Tip: The word **envelope** comes from France.

even *adjective*

An **even** number is a number that you can divide by two, with nothing left over.
*Four is an **even** number.*

every *adjective*

You use **every** to mean all the people or things in a group.
***Every** pupil in the school was there.*

excited *adjective*

If you are **excited**, you are very happy about something and you keep thinking about it.
*He was very **excited** about the party.*

exciting *adjective*

If something is **exciting**, it makes you feel very happy about it.
*This is such an **exciting** story.*

exercise *noun*

When you do **exercise**, you move your body so that you can keep healthy and strong.
*Doing sports is good **exercise**.*

eye *noun*

Your **eyes** are the parts of your body that you see with.
*I opened my **eyes** and looked around the room.*

a b c d e f g h i j k l m n o p q r s t u v w x y z

Ff

face *noun*

Your **face** is the front part of your head.
*She has a beautiful **face**.*

fair *adjective*

If something is **fair**, it seems right because it is the same for everyone.
*It's not **fair** – he's got more than me!*

> *Tip:* Some words that rhyme with **fair**:
> air   chair   hair   pair

fairy *noun*

In stories, **fairies** are tiny creatures with wings who can do magic.

fall *verb*

If a person or thing **falls**, they move towards the ground suddenly by accident.
*Be careful you don't **fall** off!*

> *Tip:* Some words that rhyme with **fall**:
> all   ball   call   tall   wall

family *noun*

A **family** is a group of people made up of parents or carers and their children. Aunts and uncles, cousins, grandmothers, and grandfathers are also part of your **family**.

fan *noun*

A **fan** is an object which blows out cool air.

> *Tip:* Some words that rhyme with **fan**:
> man   pan   plan   ran   van

farm *noun*

A **farm** is a piece of land with buildings on it where people grow crops and keep animals.

farmer *noun*

A **farmer** is a person who grows crops and keeps animals on a farm.

fast *adjective*

Something that is **fast** can move quickly.
*This car is very **fast**.*

fat *adjective*

Someone who is **fat** has a big, round body.

> *Tip:* Some words that rhyme with **fat**:
> bat   cat   hat   mat   rat

A B C D E F G H I J K L M N O P Q R S T U V W X Y Z

favourite adjective

Your **favourite** person or thing is the one you like best.
*My **favourite** food is cheese.*

feather noun

Feathers are the soft, light things that cover a bird's body. They keep the bird warm and help it to fly.

feel verb

The way you **feel**, for example happy or sad, or cold or tired, is how you are at the time.
*I **feel** very upset.*

fence noun

A **fence** is a wall made of wood or metal that goes round a piece of land.
*There is a **fence** round the garden.*

ferry noun

A **ferry** is a boat which carries people and sometimes their cars across a river or the sea.
*We went on the **ferry** to France.*

field noun

A **field** is a piece of land where people grow crops or keep animals.

film noun

A **film** is a story told in moving pictures that you watch on a screen.

finger noun

Your **fingers** are the long thin parts at the end of each hand.
*She put a ring on her **finger**.*

fire noun

Fire is the hot, bright flames that come from something that is burning.
*The **fire** destroyed the forest.*

fire engine noun

A **fire engine** is a large truck that carries

people and equipment to stop fires.

fireworks noun

Fireworks are things that make a loud bang or flashes of bright colour when they are burned.

> Tip: The word **fireworks** is made up of two words: "fire" and "works".

first adjective

If a person or thing is **first**, they come before all the others.
*January is the **first** month of the year.*

fish noun

A **fish** is an animal that lives in water.
Fish have fins to help them swim.

a b c d e f g h i j k l m n o p q r s t u v w x y z

flag *noun*

A **flag** is a piece of cloth with a pattern on it. Each country of the world has its own **flag**.

flamingo *noun*

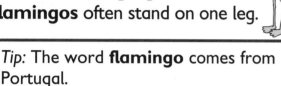

A **flamingo** is a bird which is pink and has long legs. **Flamingos** often stand on one leg.

> *Tip:* The word **flamingo** comes from Portugal.

floor *noun*

A **floor** is the part of a room that you walk on.
There were carpets on the floor.

flower *noun*

A **flower** is the part of a plant that makes seeds. **Flowers** often have bright colours and a nice smell.

fly *verb*

When a bird or aeroplane **flies**, it moves through the air.

> *Tip:* Some words that rhyme with **fly**:
> **by   cry   dry   my   sky   try   why**

fly *noun*

A **fly** is a small insect with two thin, clear wings.

food *noun*

Food is what people and animals eat.

foot *noun*

Your **feet** are the parts of your body that are at the ends of your legs, and that you stand on.
Stand with one foot in front of the other.

football *noun*

1 **Football** is a game played by two teams who kick a ball and try to score goals by getting the ball into a net.
2 A **football** is the ball that you use to play football.

> *Tip:* The word **football** is made up of two words: "foot" and "ball".

forest *noun*

A **forest** is a place where a lot of trees grow close together.

fork *noun*

A **fork** is a tool with three or four thin, sharp points that you use to eat food with.

fox *noun*

A **fox** is a wild animal that looks like a dog with red fur and a long, thick tail.

free *adjective*

If something is **free**, you can have it without paying any money for it.
*The lady gave me a **free** cake.*

> *Tip:* Some words that rhyme with **free**:
> bee   knee   see   three   tree

fridge *noun*

A **fridge** is a cupboard that uses electricity to keep food cold and fresh.
*Put the butter in the **fridge**.*

friend *noun*

A **friend** is someone you know and like, and who likes you too.

> *Tip:* You do not say the "i" in the word **friend**. It sounds like **bend**.

frog *noun*

A **frog** is a small animal with big eyes and long back legs that it uses for jumping. **Frogs** live near water.

> *Tip:* Some words that rhyme with **frog**:
> bog   dog   fog   log

frosty *adjective*

When it is **frosty**, the ground is covered in a white powder like ice because the weather is very cold.
*It was **frosty** this morning.*

fruit *noun*

Fruit is the part of a plant or a tree that has the seeds in it. You can eat many **fruits**, for example apples, bananas, and strawberries.

full *adjective*

If something is **full**, it has so much in it that it cannot hold any more.
*The glass is **full**.*

fun *noun*

When you have **fun**, you enjoy doing something and you feel happy.
*They had **fun** at the seaside.*

> *Tip:* Some words that rhyme with **fun**:
> bun   gun   run   sun

fur *noun*

Fur is the soft hair that covers the bodies of many animals.
*Pandas have black and white **fur**.*

a b c d e **f** g h i j k l m n o p q r s t u v w x y z

Gg

game *noun*

1 A **game** is something you play that has rules, for example football.

2 Children also play a **game** when they pretend to be other people.
*We played a **game** of pirates.*

Tip: Some words that rhyme with **game**:
name   same   shame   tame

garage *noun*

1 A **garage** is a building where you keep a car.

2 A **garage** is also a place where you can get your car repaired.

garden *noun*

A **garden** is a piece of land near a house where people can grow grass, flowers, and vegetables.

gate *noun*

A **gate** is a kind of door in a wall, a fence, or a hedge.

Tip: Some words that rhyme with **gate**:
date   hate   late   plate

get *verb*

1 You can use **get** to mean the same as "become".
*We will go when it starts to **get** dark.*

2 If you **get** something, someone gives it to you.
*I hope I **get** a bike for my birthday.*

3 If you **get** something, you go to where it is and bring it back.
*He went to **get** a cup of coffee.*

Tip: Some words that rhyme with **get**:
bet   net   pet   vet   wet

ghost *noun*

A **ghost** is a dead person who some people think they can see and hear.

Tip: You do not say the "h" in the word **ghost**. It sounds like **most**.

giant *noun*

In fairy stories, a **giant** is someone who is very large and very strong.

giraffe *noun*

A **giraffe** is a very tall animal with a long neck, long legs, and dark spots on its body.

Tip: The word **giraffe** comes from Italy.

girl *noun*

A **girl** is a child or a young person who is a female.

give *verb*

If you **give** someone something, you let them have it to keep.
*We always **give** her flowers on Sunday.*

glass *noun*

1 **Glass** is a hard, clear material that is used to make things like windows and bottles. It is quite easy to break **glass**.
*The salad was in a **glass** bowl.*

2 A **glass** is also a container made from **glass** that you can drink out of.
*He filled his **glass** with milk.*

> *Tip:* Some words that rhyme with **glass**:
> **brass** **class** **grass** **pass**

glasses *noun*

Glasses are two pieces of plastic or glass in a frame that people wear in front of their eyes to help them to see better.

glove *noun*

Gloves are things that you wear over your hands to keep them warm. **Gloves** have one part for your thumb and one part for each of your fingers.

glue *noun*

You use **glue** to stick things together.

go *verb*

If you **go** somewhere, you move there from another place.
*Can we **go** to the park?*

goal *noun*

In games like football, the **goal** is the place that you try to get the ball into to score a point.

goat *noun*

A **goat** is an animal about the size of a sheep. Some **goats** have horns, and hair on their chin that looks like a beard.

> *Tip:* Some words that rhyme with **goat**:
> **boat** **coat** **float** **moat** **stoat**

gold *noun*

Gold is a valuable, yellow metal that is used to make things like rings and necklaces, and also coins.

> *Tip:* Some words that rhyme with **gold**:
> **cold** **fold** **old** **sold** **told**

goldfish *noun*

A **goldfish** is a small orange fish that people often keep as a pet.

Tip: The word **goldfish** is made up of two words: "gold" and "fish".

good *adjective*

1 If you say that something is **good**, you like it.
That was a good film.

2 If you are **good**, you behave well.
Be good while I am out.

3 If you are **good** at something, you do it well.
She is good at drawing.

goose *noun*

A **goose** is a large bird with a long neck that lives near water.

grape *noun*

A **grape** is a small, round, green or purple fruit which grows in bunches.

grass *noun*

Grass is a green plant with very thin leaves that cover the ground in fields and gardens.

Tip: Some words that rhyme with **grass**:
brass   **class**   **glass**   **pass**

grasshopper *noun*

A **grasshopper** is an insect with long back legs that can jump well.

Tip: The word **grasshopper** is made up of two words: "grass" and "hopper".

great *adjective*

If you say that something is **great**, you mean that it is very good.
We had a great time.

green *noun*

Green is the colour of grass or leaves.
Her dress is green.

➜ *Look at page 78 for more colours.*

grey *noun*

Grey is a mixture of black and white, like the colour of clouds when rain is falling.

➜ *Look at page 78 for more colours.*

guinea pig *noun*

A **guinea pig** is a small animal with fur and no tail that people often keep as a pet.

guitar *noun*

A **guitar** is an instrument with strings that you play by pressing the strings with one hand and pulling them with the other hand.

Hh

hair *noun*

Hair is the soft, fine threads that grow on your head and on the bodies of many animals.
*I wash my **hair** every night.*

Tip: Some words that rhyme with **hair**:
air   **chair**   **fair**   **pair**

half *noun*

A **half** is one of two equal parts that make up a whole thing.
*We each had **half** of the cake.*

hammer *noun*

A **hammer** is a tool that is used for hitting things.

hamster *noun*

A **hamster** is a small animal that looks like a fat mouse with a short tail. People often keep **hamsters** as pets.
*She called her **hamster** Olly.*

hand *noun*

Your **hands** are the parts of your body that are at the ends of your arms, and that you use to hold things.
A **hand** has four fingers and a thumb.
*I put my **hand** in my pocket and took out the letter.*

Tip: Some words that rhyme with **hand**:
and   **band**   **land**   **sand**   **stand**

handbag *noun*

A **handbag** is a small bag used for carrying things like money and keys.

Tip: The word **handbag** is made up of two words: "hand" and "bag".

happy *adjective*

When you are **happy**, you feel pleased about something.
*They are **happy** to see each other.*

hard *adjective*

1 Something that is **hard** is solid, and it is not easy to bend it or break it.
*The glass broke on the **hard** floor.*
2 If something is **hard**, you have to try a lot to do it or to understand it.
*This puzzle is quite **hard**.*

hat *noun*

A **hat** is something that you can wear on your head.

Tip: Some words that rhyme with **hat**:
bat   **cat**   **fat**   **mat**   **rat**

hate *verb*

If you **hate** a person or a thing, you feel that you do not like them at all.
*I **hate** onions.*

Tip: Some words that rhyme with **hate**:
date   **gate**   **late**   **plate**

have *verb*

1 If you **have** something, it belongs to you.
*Do you **have** any pets?*
2 When you **have** something, you feel it, or it happens to you.
*I **have** a bad cold.*

head *noun*

Your **head** is the part of your body at the top that has your eyes, ears, nose, mouth, and brain in it.
*The ball hit him on the **head**.*

heart *noun*

Your **heart** is the part inside you which makes the blood move around your body.
*He was excited and his **heart** was beating fast.*

hedgehog *noun*

A **hedgehog** is a small animal with sharp spikes all over its back.

Tip: The word **hedgehog** is made up of two words: "hedge" and "hog".

helicopter *noun*

A **helicopter** is a small aircraft with long blades on top that go round very quickly. **Helicopters** can fly straight up and down and stay in one place in the air.

helmet *noun*

A **helmet** is a hard hat that people wear to protect their head.
*You must wear a **helmet** on your bike.*

help *verb*

If you **help** someone, you make it easier for them to do something.
*Can you **help** me tidy up?*

hen *noun*

A **hen** is a chicken that is a female. People often eat **hens'** eggs as food.

Tip: Some words that rhyme with **hen**:
den   **men**   **pen**   **ten**   **when**

hide *verb*

If you **hide** something, you put it where no one can see it or find it.
*Let's **hide** it behind the wall.*

hill *noun*

A **hill** is a piece of land that is higher than the land around it. **Hills** are not as high as mountains.
*The road went up the **hill**.*

> *Tip:* Some words that rhyme with **hill**:
> **bill   ill   pill   still   will**

hippopotamus *noun*

A **hippopotamus** is a large animal with short legs and thick skin that lives near water. Many people use the word **hippo** for short.

> *Tip:* The word **hippopotamus** comes from Greece and means "river horse".

hit *verb*

If you **hit** something, you touch it with a lot of strength.

> *Tip:* Some words that rhyme with **hit**:
> **bit   fit   kit   lit   sit**

hole *noun*

A **hole** is a gap or a hollow place in something.
*We dug a **hole** in the ground.*

holiday *noun*

A **holiday** is a time when you do not need to work or go to school.
*Where are you going on **holiday**?*

home *noun*

Your **home** is the place where you live.
*We stayed at **home** and watched TV.*

homework *noun*

Homework is work that a teacher gives you to do at home.
*I have done all of my **homework**.*

> *Tip:* The word **homework** is made up of two words: "home" and "work".

honey *noun*

Honey is a sweet, very thick liquid that is made by bees. You can eat **honey** on bread.

hop *verb*

If you **hop**, you jump on one foot.

> *Tip:* Some words that rhyme with **hop**:
> **mop   pop   shop   stop   top**

a b c d e f **g** **h** i j k l m n o p q r s t u v w x y z

horrible *adjective*

If something is **horrible**, it is very nasty.
*There was a **horrible** smell.*

horse *noun*

A **horse** is a large animal with a long tail and four legs. People ride on **horses** or use them to pull things along.

hospital *noun*

A **hospital** is a building where doctors and nurses care for people who are ill or hurt.

hot *adjective*

If something is **hot**, it is very warm.
*Don't touch the plate - it's **hot**.*

> *Tip:* Some words that rhyme with **hot**:
> **cot   got   not   pot   spot**

house *noun*

A **house** is a building where people live.
*Come to my **house** for dinner.*

hug *verb*

When you **hug** someone, you put your arms around them and hold them close to you.
*I like my mum to **hug** me when she reads a story.*

> *Tip:* Some words that rhyme with **hug**:
> **bug   jug   mug   rug   slug**

huge *adjective*

Something that is **huge** is very big.
*Elephants are **huge** animals.*

hungry *adjective*

If you are **hungry**, you want to eat something.

hurt *verb*

If you **hurt** someone or something, you make them feel pain.
*I fell over and **hurt** my leg yesterday.*

Ii

ice *noun*

Ice is water that has frozen. It is very cold and hard.
*The ground was covered with **ice**.*

> *Tip:* Some words that rhyme with **ice**:
> **dice   mice   nice   rice   twice**

ice cream *noun*

Ice cream is a very cold, sweet food that is made from frozen milk or cream.

icicle *noun*

An **icicle** is a long piece of ice with a point at the end that hangs down from something. **Icicles** are made from dripping water that has frozen.

idea *noun*

An **idea** is something new that you have thought of.
*He had an **idea** for a story.*

igloo *noun*

An **igloo** is a house made out of bricks of snow.

ill *adjective*

When you are **ill**, you do not feel well.
*He is too **ill** to go to school.*

> *Tip:* Some words that rhyme with **ill**:
> **bill   hill   pill   still   will**

ink *noun*

Ink is a liquid that you use to write or print with. Pens have **ink** inside them.

> *Tip:* Some words that rhyme with **ink**:
> **drink   pink   sink   think   wink**

insect *noun*

An **insect** is a small animal with six legs, for example a bee or a beetle. Many **insects** have wings and can fly.

A
B
C
D
E
F
G
H
I
J
K
L
M
N
O
P
Q
R
S
T
U
V
W
X
Y
Z

inside

1 If something is **inside** another thing, it is in it.
*What's **inside** the box?*

2 **Inside** also means indoors.
*He went **inside** and locked the door.*

Tip: The word **inside** is made up of two words: "in" and "side".

instrument *noun*

An **instrument** is something, for example a piano or a guitar, which you use to make music.
*He plays three **instruments**, including the violin.*

interesting *adjective*

If something is **interesting**, you want to know more about it.
*What an **interesting** book!*

internet *noun*

The **internet** is something that joins a computer to other computers all over the world. You send emails using the **internet**.

invitation *noun*

If you get an **invitation**, someone asks you to come to something like a party.
*I gave him an **invitation** to my party.*

invite *verb*

If you **invite** someone to something, for example a party, you ask them to come to it.

iron *noun*

An **iron** is a piece of equipment with a flat bottom that gets hot. You move the bottom of the **iron** over clothes to make them smooth.

island *noun*

An **island** is a piece of land that has water all around it.

Tip: You do not say the "s" in the word **island**.

Jj

jacket *noun*
A **jacket** is a short coat.

jam *noun*
Jam is a soft, sweet food that is made from fruit and sugar.

jeans *noun*
Jeans are blue trousers with pockets at the front and back.
*Everyone wore **jeans** and a T-shirt.*

jelly *noun*
Jelly is a sweet food that wobbles.
*We had raspberry **jelly** and ice cream.*

jellyfish *noun*
A **jellyfish** has a clear soft body and lives in the sea. They can sting you.

> *Tip:* The word **jellyfish** is made up of two words: "jelly" and "fish".

jigsaw *noun*
A **jigsaw** is a picture on cardboard that has been cut up into pieces. You have to fit them together again.

job *noun*
A **job** is the work that a person does to earn money.
*My sister wants to get a **job**.*

joke *noun*
A **joke** is something that someone says to make you laugh.

jug *noun*
A **jug** is a container with a handle. You use a **jug** for pouring liquids.

> *Tip:* Some words that rhyme with **jug**:
> **bug   hug   mug   rug   slug**

juice *noun*
Juice is the liquid from a fruit or vegetable.
*He had a large glass of fresh orange **juice**.*

jump *verb*
When you **jump**, you bend your knees and push yourself into the air.

> *Tip:* Some words that rhyme with **jump**:
> **bump   hump   lump   plump**

jumper *noun*
You wear a **jumper** to keep yourself warm. It has sleeves and covers the top half of your body.
*She had her favourite **jumper** on.*

a b c d e f g h i **j** k l m n o p q r s t u v w x y z

Kk

kangaroo *noun*

A **kangaroo** is a large Australian animal that carries its babies in a pouch on its stomach.

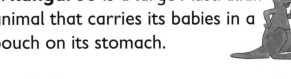

key *noun*

A **key** is a piece of metal that opens or closes a lock.

kick *verb*

If you **kick** something, you hit it with your foot.
*How hard can you **kick** the ball?*

> *Tip:* Some words that rhyme with **kick**:
> **lick   sick   stick   tick   trick**

king *noun*

A **king** is a man who rules a country.

> *Tip:* Some words that rhyme with **king**:
> **ring   sing   sting   thing   wing**

kiss *verb*

If you **kiss** someone, you touch them with your lips.
*She went to **kiss** him goodbye at the door.*

kitchen *noun*

A **kitchen** is a room that is used for cooking.

kite *noun*

A **kite** is a toy that you fly in the wind at the end of a long string.

kitten *noun*

A **kitten** is a very young cat.

knee *noun*

Your **knee** is the part in the middle of your leg where it bends.

> *Tip:* You do not say the "k" in the word **knee**. It sounds like **bee**.

knife *noun*

A **knife** is a sharp metal tool that you use to cut things.

> *Tip:* You do not say the "k" in the word **knife**. It sounds like **wife**.

knight *noun*

In the past, a **knight** was a soldier who rode a horse.

> *Tip:* You do not say the "k" in the word **knight**. It sounds like **night**.

koala *noun*

A **koala** is an animal that looks like a small bear with grey fur.

Ll

ladder *noun*

A **ladder** is a set of steps that you can move around. You use it for reaching high places.
*He climbed the **ladder** to see over the wall.*

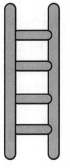

ladybird *noun*

A **ladybird** is a small round beetle that has red wings with black spots.

> *Tip:* The word **ladybird** is made up of two words: "lady" and "bird".

lake *noun*

A **lake** is an area of water with land around it.

> *Tip:* Some words that rhyme with **lake**:
> **bake   cake   make   snake   take**

lamb *noun*

A **lamb** is a young sheep.

> *Tip:* You do not say the "b" in the word **lamb**. It sounds like **jam**.

last *adjective*

The **last** thing or person comes after all the others.
*I read the **last** three pages of the chapter.*

late

Late means after the proper time.
*We arrived **late** for our class.*

> *Tip:* Some words that rhyme with **late**:
> **date   gate   hate   plate**

laugh *verb*

When you **laugh**, you smile and make a sound because something is funny.
*The boys all started to **laugh** at his joke.*

leaf *noun*

The **leaves** of a plant are the parts that are flat, thin, and usually green.
*A green **leaf** floated on the water.*

left *adjective*

The **left** side of something is one side of it. For example, English writing begins on the **left** side of the page.
*I hurt my **left** knee when I fell.*

leg *noun*

A person's or animal's **legs** are the long parts of their body that they use for walking and standing.
*Stand with your **legs** apart.*

a b c d e f g h i j k **l** m n o p q r s t u v w x y z

lemon *noun*

A **lemon** is a yellow fruit with very sour juice.

leopard *noun*

A **leopard** is a large, wild cat with yellow fur and black spots.

letter *noun*

1 A **letter** is a message on paper that you post to someone.
*I received a **letter** from a friend.*

2 **Letters** are shapes that you write to make words.
*'Cat' starts with the **letter** 'c'.*

lick *verb*

If you **lick** something, you move your tongue over it.
***Lick** your ice cream before it drips.*

> *Tip:* Some words that rhyme with **lick**:
> **kick   sick   stick   tick   trick**

lid *noun*

A **lid** is the top of a container that you can remove.
*She lifted the **lid** of the box.*

light *noun*

A **light** is something like a lamp, that allows you to see.

> *Tip:* Some words that rhyme with **light**:
> **fight   knight   night   right   tight**

like *verb*

If you **like** something, you think it is nice or interesting.
*Do you **like** swimming?*

lion *noun*

A **lion** is a large wild cat that lives in Africa. **Lions** have yellow fur, and male **lions** have long hair on their head and neck.

lip *noun*

Your **lips** are the edges of your mouth.
*He bit his **lip**.*

> *Tip:* Some words that rhyme with **lip**:
> **chip   nip   ship   skip   zip**

litter *noun*

Litter is rubbish that people drop in the street.
*Please don't drop any **litter**.*

little *adjective*

A person or thing that is **little** is small in size.
*They live in a **little** house.*

live *verb*

You **live** in the place where your home is.
*Where do you **live**?*

> *Tip:* When **live** means where your home is, it sounds like **give**.

living room *noun*

The **living room** in a house is the room where the family spend a lot of time.
Our TV is in the corner of the living room.

lizard *noun*

A **lizard** is a small reptile with a long tail and rough skin.

log *noun*

A **log** is a thick piece of wood from a tree.

> *Tip:* Some words that rhyme with **log**:
> **bog**   **dog**   **fog**   **frog**

lolly *noun*

A **lolly** is a sweet or ice cream on a stick.

long *adjective*

Something that is **long** measures a great distance from one end to the other.
There is a long table in the kitchen.

look *verb*

When you **look** at something, you turn your eyes so that you can see it.
Look out the window!

> *Tip:* Some words that rhyme with **look**:
> **book   cook   hook   shook   took**

lorry *noun*

A **lorry** is a large vehicle for moving things by road.

loud *adjective*

A **loud** noise is a very big sound.
The music was very loud.

love *verb*

1 If you **love** someone, you care very much about them.
   I love my dad.
2 If you **love** something, you like it very much.
   We both love football.

lovely *adjective*

A **lovely** thing or person is very beautiful or very nice.
I thought she looked lovely.

lunch *noun*

Lunch is the meal that you have in the middle of the day.

a b c d e f g h i j k l m n o p q r s t u v w x y z

Mm

magic *noun*

In stories, **magic** is a special power that allows you to do impossible things.

make *verb*

1 If you **make** something, you put it together or build it from other things.
*They **make** all their own clothes.*

2 If you **make** a person do something, they must do it.
*My parents **make** me tidy my room.*

> *Tip:* Some words that rhyme with **make**:
> **bake   cake   lake   snake   take**

man *noun*

A **man** is an adult male person.

> *Tip:* Some words that rhyme with **man**:
> **fan   pan   plan   ran   van**

map *noun*

A **map** is a drawing of an area from above. It shows where the towns, roads, rivers and railways are.

mat *noun*

A **mat** is a small piece of cloth, wood, or plastic that you put on a table or on the floor to protect it.
*The cat is sleeping on the red **mat**.*

meat *noun*

Meat is the part of an animal that people cook and eat.
*I don't eat **meat** or fish.*

> *Tip:* Some words that rhyme with **meat**:
> **eat   heat   neat   seat   treat**

milk *noun*

Milk is the white liquid that all baby mammals get from their mothers. People also drink **milk** that farmers get from cows and goats.
*They make cheese from goat's **milk** too.*

mirror *noun*

A **mirror** is a piece of shiny glass in which you can see yourself.

money *noun*

Money is what you use to buy things.
*Cars cost a lot of **money**.*

monkey *noun*

A **monkey** is an animal that has a long tail and can climb trees.

monster *noun*

In stories, a **monster** is a big, ugly creature that frightens people.

month *noun*

A **month** is one part of a year. There are twelve **months** in one year.
*We are going on holiday next **month**.*

➜ *Look at page 79 for more about **days and months**.*

moon *noun*

The **moon** shines in the sky at night and moves around the earth every month.

mop *noun*

A **mop** has a long handle with a sponge or strings on the end. You use a **mop** to wash the floor.

> *Tip:* Some words that rhyme with **mop**:
> **hop   pop   shop   stop   top**

morning *noun*

The **morning** is the early part of the day, before lunch.
*What do you want to do in the **morning**?*

motorbike *noun*

A **motorbike** is a large bike with an engine.

> *Tip:* The word **motorbike** is made up of two words: "motor" and "bike".

mountain *noun*

A **mountain** is a very high area of land with steep sides.

mouse *noun*

1 A **mouse** is a small animal with a long tail.
2 You use a **mouse** to move things on a computer screen.

mouth *noun*

Your **mouth** is the part of your face that you use for eating or talking.

mud *noun*

Mud is a mixture of earth and water. *There was **mud** on my football boots.*

mug *noun*

A **mug** is a deep cup with straight sides.
*He poured tea into the **mugs**.*

> *Tip:* Some words that rhyme with **mug**:
> **bug   hug   jug   rug   slug**

mushroom *noun*

A **mushroom** is a plant with a short stem and a round top that you can eat.

music *noun*

Music is the sound that you make when you sing or play instruments.
*What's your favourite **music**?*

a b c d e f g h i j k l **m** n o p q r s t u v w x y z

Nn

nail *noun*

1 A **nail** is a thin piece of metal. It is flat at one end and it has a point at the other end.
A picture hung on a nail in the wall.

2 Your **nails** are the thin hard parts that grow at the ends of your fingers and toes.
Try to keep your nails short.

Tip: Some words that rhyme with **nail**:
pail   rail   sail   snail   tail

name *noun*

A person's **name** is the word or words that you use to talk to them, or to talk about them.
Is your name Peter?

Tip: Some words that rhyme with **name**:
game   same   shame   tame

naughty *adjective*

A **naughty** child does things which are bad.
She was so naughty, her mother sent her to bed early.

neck *noun*

Your **neck** is the part of your body between your head and the rest of your body.

necklace *noun*

A **necklace** is a chain of beads or jewels that you wear around your neck.
She's wearing a beautiful necklace.

Tip: The word **necklace** is made up of two words: "neck" and "lace".

needle *noun*

A **needle** is a small, thin metal tool with a sharp point that you use for sewing.
I used a needle and thread to sew the button on.

nest *noun*

A **nest** is the place where a bird keeps its eggs or its babies.
There were three eggs in the bird's nest.

Tip: Some words that rhyme with **nest**:
best   test   vest   west

net *noun*

A **net** is made from pieces of string or rope tied together with holes between them.

Tip: Some words that rhyme with **net**:
bet   get   pet   vet   wet

new *adjective*

If something is **new**, nobody has used it before.
*I am wearing my **new** shoes.*

nice *adjective*

If something is **nice**, you like it.
*They live in a really **nice** house.*

Tip: Some words that rhyme with **nice**:
dice   ice   mice   rice   twice

night *noun*

The **night** is the time when it is dark outside, and most people sleep.
*The party went on until late at **night**.*

Tip: Some words that rhyme with **night**:
fight   knight   light   right   tight

no

You use **no** to say that something is not true or to refuse something.
*"Do you want a drink?"—"**No**, thank you."*

nose *noun*

Your **nose** is the part of your face above your mouth that you use for breathing and for noticing smells.
*He sneezed and blew his **nose**.*

now

You use **now** to talk about the present time.
*I must go **now**.*

Tip: Some words that rhyme with **now**:
bow   cow   how   wow

number *noun*

A **number** is a word that you use to count.
*What **number** is your house?*

→ *Look at page 80 for some **numbers**.*

nurse *noun*

A **nurse** is a person whose job is to care for people who are ill.
*She thanked the **nurses** at the hospital.*

nursery *noun*

A **nursery** is a place where young children go to play and learn during the day.
*My little brother goes to **nursery**.*

nut *noun*

A **nut** is a dry fruit with a hard shell.
***Nuts** and seeds are very good for you.*

Tip: Some words that rhyme with **nut**:
but   cut   hut   shut

a b c d e f g h i j k l **m** n o p q r s t u v w x y z

Oo

octopus *noun*

An **octopus** is a soft ocean animal with eight long arms.

odd *adjective*

Odd numbers are numbers that cannot be divided by the number two.

off

1 If you take something **off** another thing, it is no longer on it.
*He took his feet **off** the desk.*

2 When something that uses electricity is **off**, it is not using electricity.
*The light was **off**.*

old *adjective*

1 An **old** person is someone who has lived for a long time.
*An **old** lady sat next to me.*

2 An **old** thing is something that somebody made a long time ago.
*We have a very **old** car.*

> *Tip:* Some words that rhyme with **old**:
> **cold**   **fold**   **gold**   **sold**   **told**

on

1 If someone or something is **on** a surface, it is resting there.
*My teddy was **on** the bed.*

2 When something that uses electricity is **on**, it is using electricity.
*The television is **on**.*

onion *noun*

An **onion** is a small, round vegetable with a very strong taste.

open *verb*

When you **open** something, or when it **opens**, it is no longer closed.
*She tried to **open** the door.*

orange *noun*

An **orange** is a round fruit with a thick skin and lots of juice.

orange *adjective*

Orange is a mixture of red and yellow.
→ *Look at page 78 for more **colours**.*

outside *adjective*

If you are **outside**, you are not in a building.

> *Tip:* The word **outside** is made up of two words: "out" and "side".

owl *noun*

An **owl** is a bird with large eyes that hunts at night.

A B C D E F G H I J K L M N O P Q R S T U V W X Y Z

Pp

page *noun*

A **page** is one side of a piece of paper in a book, a magazine, or a newspaper. *Turn to* **page** *4.*

paint *noun*

Paint is a liquid used to decorate buildings, or to make a picture.
Can I use some of your blue **paint**?

paint *verb*

If you **paint** something on a piece of paper or cloth, you make a picture of it using **paint**.
He likes to **paint** *flowers.*

pair *noun*

A **pair** of things is two things of the same size and shape that are used together.
Mrs McDonald wore a **pair** *of plain black shoes.*

Tip: Some words that rhyme with **pair**:
air   chair   fair   hair

pan *noun*

A **pan** is a container with a long handle that is used for cooking.

Tip: Some words that rhyme with **pan**:
fan   man   plan   ran   van

panda *noun*

A **panda** is a large animal with black and white fur.

Tip: The Chinese word for **panda** means "bear cat".

paper *noun*

1 **Paper** is a material that you write on or wrap things with.
He wrote his name on a piece of **paper**.

2 A **paper** is a newspaper.

park *noun*

A **park** is a place with grass and trees. People go to **parks** to take exercise or play games.

parrot *noun*

A **parrot** is a bird with a curved beak and bright feathers.

party *noun*

A **party** is a time when people meet to have fun.
She's having a ***party***.

pasta *noun*

Pasta is made from a mixture of flour, eggs, and water.
I love ***pasta*** *and vegetables.*

> *Tip:* The word **pasta** comes from Italy.

paw *noun*

The **paws** of an animal such as a cat, dog, or bear are its feet.
The kitten was black with white ***paws***.

peach *noun*

A **peach** is a round fruit with a soft red and orange skin.

peanut *noun*

Peanuts are small nuts that you can eat.

> *Tip:* The word **peanut** is made up of two words: "pea" and "nut".

pear *noun*

A **pear** is a fruit which is narrow at the top and wide and round at the bottom.

peas *noun*

Peas are small, round, green vegetables.

peg *noun*

A **peg** is a small piece of metal or wood on a wall that you hang things on.
Please hang your coat on the ***peg***.

pen *noun*

A **pen** is a long thin tool that you use for writing with ink.

> *Tip:* Some words that rhyme with **pen**:
> den   hen   men   ten   when

pencil *noun*

A **pencil** is a thin piece of wood with a material in it that you use to write or draw with.

penguin *noun*

A **penguin** is a black and white bird that lives in very cold places. **Penguins** can swim but they cannot fly.

pepper *noun*

1 **Pepper** is a powder with a hot taste that you put on food.
2 A **pepper** is a green, red or yellow vegetable with seeds inside it.

pet *noun*

A **pet** is a tame animal that you keep in your home.

> *Tip:* Some words that rhyme with **pet**:
> bet   get   net   vet   wet

phone *noun*

A **phone** is a piece of equipment which you use to talk to someone in another place.
*Two minutes later the **phone** rang.*

photograph *noun*

A **photograph** is a picture that you take with a camera. Many people use the word **photo** for short.
*She took **photographs** of her friends.*

> *Tip:* The word **photograph** is made up of two words: "photo" and "graph".

piano *noun*

A **piano** is a large instrument for playing music. You play it by pressing the black and white keys.

> *Tip:* The word **piano** comes from Italy.

picnic *noun*

When people have a **picnic**, they eat a meal outside, usually in a park or a forest, or at the beach.
*We're going on a **picnic** tomorrow.*

picture *noun*

A **picture** is a drawing or painting.

pig *noun*

A **pig** is a farm animal with a fat body and short legs.

> *Tip:* Some words that rhyme with **pig**:
> **big**　　**dig**　　**tig**　　**twig**　　**wig**

pillow *noun*

A **pillow** is something soft that you rest your head on when you are in bed.

pin *noun*

A **pin** is a very small thin piece of metal with a point at one end.
*We fastened it on with a **pin**.*

> *Tip:* Some words that rhyme with **pin**:
> **bin**　　**chin**　　**tin**　　**twin**　　**win**

pineapple *noun*

A **pineapple** is a large sweet yellow fruit with a lot of juice. Its skin is brown, thick, and very rough.

> *Tip:* The word **pineapple** is made up of two words: "pine" and "apple".

pink *adjective*

Pink is a colour between white and red.
*My new dress is **pink**.*

> *Tip:* Some words that rhyme with **pink**:
> **ink**　　**drink**　　**sink**　　**think**　　**wink**

➜ *Look at page 78 for more **colours**.*

a b c d e f g h i j k l m n o p q r s t u v w x y z

A B C D E F G H I J K L M N O P Q R S T U V W X Y Z

pirate *noun*

Pirates are people who attack ships and steal things from them.
The pirates have hidden the gold.

pizza *noun*

A **pizza** is a flat, round piece of bread. **Pizzas** are covered with cheese, tomatoes, and other toppings.

> *Tip:* The word **pizza** comes from Italy.

plane *noun*

A **plane** is a large vehicle with wings and engines that flies through the air.

planet *noun*

You find **planets** in space. They move around stars. The Earth is a **planet**.

plant *noun*

A **plant** is a living thing that grows in the earth. **Plants** have a stem, leaves, and roots.

plate *noun*

A **plate** is a flat dish that is used for holding food.
She pushed her plate away.

> *Tip:* Some words that rhyme with **plate**:
> **date   gate   hate   late**

play *verb*

1 When you **play**, you spend time using toys and taking part in games. *She likes to play with the ball.*

2 If you **play** an instrument, you make music with it.

> *Tip:* Some words that rhyme with **play**:
> **away   day   may   say   way**

playground *noun*

A **playground** is a special area where children can play.

> *Tip:* The word **playground** is made up of two words: "play" and "ground".

please

You say **please** when you are asking someone to do something.
Can you help us, please?

plum *noun*

A **plum** is a small fruit which usually has a dark red skin.

polar bear *noun*

A **polar bear** is a large white bear which lives in the area around the North Pole.

police *noun*

The **police** are the people who make sure that we all obey the law.

pond *noun*

A **pond** is a small area of water.
We can feed the ducks on the pond.

pony *noun*

A **pony** is a small horse.

potato *noun*

Potatoes are hard round white vegetables with brown or red skins. They grow under the ground.
My favourite meal is sausages with mashed potatoes.

Tip: The word **potato** comes from Spain.

pram *noun*

A **pram** is a small bed on wheels that a baby can be pushed around in.
The baby is sleeping in his pram.

present *noun*

A **present** is something that you give to someone for them to keep.
She got a present for her birthday.

pretty *adjective*

If something is **pretty**, it is nice to look at.
She was wearing a pretty necklace.

prince *noun*

A **prince** is a boy or a man in the family of a king or queen.

princess *noun*

A **princess** is a girl or a woman in the family of a king or queen.

puddle *noun*

A **puddle** is a small amount of water on the ground.
Splashing in puddles is lots of fun.

pull *verb*

When you **pull** something, you hold it and move it towards you.
She was trying to pull her socks off.

puppy *noun*

A **puppy** is a young dog.

purple *noun*

Purple is a mixture of red and blue.
Some grapes are purple.

→ *Look at page 78 for more colours.*

a b c d e f g h i j k l m n o **p** q r s t u v w x y z

purse *noun*

A **purse** is a small bag that women use to carry money and other things.
*Lauren reached in her **purse** for her money.*

push *verb*

When you **push** something, you press it in order to move it away from you.
*I started to **push** back my chair and stand up.*

put *verb*

When you **put** something somewhere, you move it there.
*Steven **put** the book on the desk.*

puzzle *noun*

A **puzzle** is a picture on cardboard that has been cut up into pieces. You have to fit them together again.
*At last I have finished the **puzzle**.*

pyjamas *noun*

Pyjamas are loose trousers and a jacket that you wear in bed.

quack *verb*

When a duck **quacks**, it makes a loud sound.

> *Tip:* Some words that rhyme with **quack**:
> **back   black   pack   sack   track**

queen *noun*

A **queen** is a woman who rules a country, or a woman who is married to a king.

question *noun*

A **question** is something that you say or write to ask about something.
*They asked **questions** about her holiday.*

quick *adjective*

Something that is **quick** moves or does things with great speed.
*The mouse was too **quick** for the cat.*

quiet *adjective*

Someone who is **quiet** makes only a little bit of noise or no noise at all.
*The baby was so **quiet** I didn't know he was there.*

A B C D E F G H I J K L M N O P Q R S T U V W X Y Z

Rr

rabbit noun

A **rabbit** is a small animal with long ears. **Rabbits** live in holes in the ground.

race noun

A **race** is a competition to see who is fastest, for example in running or driving.

radio noun

A **radio** is a piece of equipment you use to hear programmes with talking, news and music.

rain noun

Rain is water that falls from the clouds in small drops.
My mother told me stay out of the rain.

rainbow noun

A **rainbow** is a half circle of different colours in the sky. You can sometimes see a **rainbow** when it rains.

> *Tip:* The word **rainbow** is made up of two words: "rain" and "bow".

raspberry noun

A **raspberry** is a small soft red fruit. **Raspberries** grow on bushes.

> *Tip:* The word **raspberry** is made up of two words: "rasp" and "berry".

rat noun

A **rat** is an animal that looks like a mouse. A **rat** has a long tail and sharp teeth.

> *Tip:* Some words that rhyme with **rat**:
>
> bat   cat   fat   hat   mat

read verb

When you **read**, you look at written words and understand them, and sometimes say them aloud.
I like her to read me a story at night.

really

1 You say **really** to show how much you mean something.
  I'm really sorry I can't come.

2 You say **really** to show that what you are saying is true.
  Are we really going to get a dog?

rectangle noun

A **rectangle** is a shape with four straight sides.

→ *Look at page 78 for more shapes.*

a b c d e f g h i j k l m n o p q **r** s t u v w x y z

red *noun*

Red is the colour of blood or a strawberry.
*Her dress is bright **red**.*

➔ *Look at page 78 for more **colours**.*

reptile *noun*

A **reptile** is an animal that has cold blood, rough skin, and lays eggs. Snakes and lizards are **reptiles**.

rhinoceros *noun*

A **rhinoceros** is a large wild animal with thick grey skin. A **rhinoceros** has one or two horns on 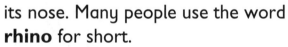 its nose. Many people use the word **rhino** for short.

> *Tip:* The word **rhinoceros** comes from Greek and means "with a nose-horn".

rice *noun*

Rice is white or brown grains from a plant. **Rice** grows in wet areas.
*The meal was chicken and **rice**.*

> *Tip:* Some words that rhyme with **rice**:
> **dice   ice   mice   nice   twice**

rich *adjective*

Someone who is **rich** has a lot of money and expensive things.
*She is a **rich** woman with a big house.*

ride *verb*

When you **ride** a horse or a bike, you sit on it and control it as it moves along.
*We watched the girl **ride** her horse.*

right *adjective*

1 If something is **right**, it is correct and there have been no mistakes.
*Only Emma knew the **right** answer.*

2 The **right** side of something is the opposite side from the left side. Most people write with their **right** hand.

> *Tip:* Some words that rhyme with **right**:
> **fight   knight   light   night   tight**

ring *noun*

A **ring** is a round piece of metal that you wear on a finger.
*He turned the **ring** on his finger.*

> *Tip:* Some words that rhyme with **ring**:
> **king   sing   sting   thing   wing**

river *noun*

A **river** is a long line of water that flows into the sea.
*This is one of the longest **rivers** in the world.*

road *noun*

A **road** is a long piece of hard ground for vehicles to travel on.
*Look both ways before you cross the **road**.*

robot *noun*

A **robot** is a machine that can move and do things that it has been told to do.
Robots can be sent to the moon.

rock *noun*

A **rock** is a large bit of stone that you can pick up.
*She threw the **rock** into the lake.*

> *Tip:* Some words that rhyme with **rock**:
> **block**   **clock**   **lock**   **sock**

rocket *noun*

A **rocket** is a vehicle that people use to travel into space.
*This is the **rocket** that went to the moon.*

roof *noun*

The **roof** of a building is the bit on top that covers it.
*Our house has a red **roof**.*

room *noun*

A **room** is a part of a building that has its own walls.

roundabout *noun*

A **roundabout** is a piece of playground equipment that children sit on to go round and round.

> *Tip:* The word **roundabout** is made up of two words: "round" and "about".

rubber *noun*

A **rubber** is a small piece of rubber used to remove pencil mistakes.
*Have you got a **rubber** I could use?*

rubbish *noun*

Rubbish is things like empty packets and used paper that you throw away.

rucksack *noun*

A **rucksack** is a small bag that you carry on your back.

rug *noun*

A **rug** is like a small carpet.

> *Tip:* Some words that rhyme with **rug**:
> **bug**   **hug**   **jug**   **mug**   **slug**

ruler *noun*

A **ruler** is a long, flat piece of wood or plastic with straight edges. You use a **ruler** for measuring things or drawing straight lines.
*You need a pencil and a **ruler** for maths.*

run *verb*

When you **run**, you move very quickly on your legs.
*He started to **run** as fast as he could.*

> *Tip:* Some words that rhyme with **run**:
> **bun**   **fun**   **gun**   **sun**

a b c d e f g h i j k l m n o p q **r** s t u v w x y z

Ss

sad *adjective*

If you are **sad**, you don't feel happy.
*I'm **sad** that he is leaving.*

> *Tip:* Some words that rhyme with **sad**:
> **bad   dad   had   mad   pad**

salad *noun*

A **salad** is a mixture of vegetables and sometimes other foods. You usually eat **salads** cold.

salt *noun*

Salt is a white powder that you use to make food taste better.
*Now add **salt** and pepper.*

sand *noun*

Sand is a powder made of very small pieces of stone. Some deserts and most beaches are made of **sand**.
*We had so much fun playing in the **sand**.*

> *Tip:* Some words that rhyme with **sand**:
> **and   band   hand   land   stand**

sandal *noun*

Sandals are light shoes that you wear in warm weather.
*He put on a pair of old **sandals**.*

sandwich *noun*

A **sandwich** is two slices of bread with another food such as cheese or meat between them.
*She ate a large **sandwich**.*

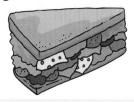

sausage *noun*

A **sausage** is a mixture of very small pieces of meat and other foods, inside a long thin skin.

saw *noun*

A **saw** is a metal tool for cutting wood.
*He used a **saw** to cut the branches off.*

scarf *noun*

A **scarf** is a piece of cloth that you wear round your neck to keep you warm.

school *noun*

A **school** is a place where people go to learn.
***School** starts at 9 o'clock.*

scissors *noun*

Scissors are a small tool for cutting with two sharp parts that are joined together.
*Cut the card using **scissors**.*

Tip: You do not say the "c" in the word **scissors**.

scooter *noun*

A **scooter** is a kind of child's bicycle. The child stands on it with one leg and uses the other leg to push themselves along.

sea *noun*

A **sea** is a large area of salt water near the land.
*They swam in the warm **sea**.*

seagull *noun*

Seagulls is the name given to black, grey and white birds that live near the sea.

Tip: The word **seagull** is made up of two words: "sea" and "gull".

seaside *noun*

The **seaside** is an area next to the sea.
*I spent a few days at the **seaside**.*

Tip: The word **seaside** is made up of two words: "sea" and "side".

seat *noun*

A **seat** is something that you can sit on.

Tip: Some words that rhyme with **seat**:
eat   heat   meat   neat   treat

see *verb*

If you **see** something, you are looking at it or you notice it.
*We couldn't **see** anything in the thick fog.*

Tip: Some words that rhyme with **see**:
bee   free   knee   three   tree

seesaw *noun*

A **seesaw** is a piece of playground equipment. A child sits on each end of a long plank and they go up and down in turn.

Tip: The word **seesaw** is made up of two words: "see" and "saw".

shape *noun*

The **shape** of something is the way its outside edges or surfaces look.

→ *Look at page 78 for some **shapes**.*

shark *noun*

A **shark** is a very large fish. **Sharks** have very sharp teeth and some have a big fin that sticks out of the water.

a b c d e f g h i j k l m n o p q r s t u v w x y z

sharpener *noun*

A **sharpener** is something you use to make your pencil sharp.
*Please may I borrow your **sharpener**?*

shed *noun*

A **shed** is a small building where you store things.
*The house has a large **shed** in the garden.*

sheep *noun*

A **sheep** is a farm animal with thick hair called wool.
Farmers keep **sheep** for their wool or for their meat.

shell *noun*

The **shell** of an animal or a sea animal is the hard part that covers its back and protects it.
*They found pretty **shells** on the beach.*

> *Tip:* Some words that rhyme with **shell:**
> **bell   fell   sell   tell   well**

ship *noun*

A **ship** is a large boat that carries people or things.
*The **ship** was ready to leave.*

> *Tip:* Some words that rhyme with **ship:**
> **chip   lip   nip   trip   zip**

shirt *noun*

A **shirt** is something you wear on the top part of your body. It has a collar and buttons.

shoe *noun*

Shoes are a type of clothing that you wear on your feet.
*I need a new pair of **shoes**.*

shop *noun*

A **shop** is a place that sells things.
*He and his wife run a clothes **shop**.*

> *Tip:* Some words that rhyme with **shop:**
> **hop   mop   pop   stop   top**

shorts *noun*

Shorts are trousers with short legs.
*He was wearing blue **shorts**.*

shower *noun*

A **shower** is a thing that you stand under, that covers you with water so you can wash yourself.
*I was in the **shower** when the phone rang.*

sick *adjective*

If you are **sick**, you are not well.
*He's very **sick** and needs a doctor.*

> *Tip:* Some words that rhyme with **sick:**
> **kick   lick   stick   tick   trick**

silly *adjective*

If you are **silly**, you do not behave in a sensible way.
*Don't be **silly**!*

sing *verb*

When you **sing**, you make music with your voice.
*I love to **sing**.*

> *Tip:* Some words that rhyme with **sing**:
> **king   ring   sting   thing   wing**

sink *noun*

A **sink** is a large fixed container in a kitchen or a bathroom that you can fill with water.
*The **sink** was filled with dirty dishes.*

> *Tip:* Some words that rhyme with **sink**:
> **ink   drink   pink   think   wink**

sister *noun*

Your **sister** is a girl or woman who has the same parents as you.

sit *verb*

If you are **sitting** in a chair, your bottom is resting on the chair and the top part of your body is straight.
*I told him to **sit** on the stool.*

> *Tip:* Some words that rhyme with **sit**:
> **bit   fit   hit   kit   knit**

skateboard *noun*

A **skateboard** is a narrow board on wheels which you stand on to ride it.
*My brother can do tricks on his **skateboard**.*

> *Tip:* The word **skateboard** is made up of two words: "skate" and "board".

skeleton *noun*

A **skeleton** is all the bones in a person's or animal's body.
*A human **skeleton** has over 200 bones.*

skip *verb*

If you **skip** somewhere, you move along jumping from one foot to the other.
*We started to **skip** down the street to school.*

> *Tip:* Some words that rhyme with **skip**:
> **chip   lip   nip   ship   zip**

skipping rope *noun*

A **skipping rope** is a long piece of rope that you can skip with.

skirt *noun*

A **skirt** is something that hangs down from the waist and covers part of the legs.
*I like your new **skirt**.*

sky *noun*

The **sky** is the space around the Earth which you can see when you look up.

> *Tip:* Some words that rhyme with **sky**:
> **by   cry   dry   fly   my   try   why**

sleep *verb*

If you **sleep**, you rest with your eyes closed and you do not move.
Be quiet! He is trying to sleep.

slide *noun*

A **slide** is a piece of playground equipment for sliding down.

slipper *noun*

Slippers are loose, soft shoes that you wear indoors.
She put on a pair of slippers.

slow *adjective*

If something is **slow**, it does not move quickly.
The bus was very slow.

slug *noun*

A **slug** is a small animal with a long soft body and no legs that moves very slowly.

> *Tip:* Some words that rhyme with **slug**:
> **bug   hug   jug   mug   rug**

small *adjective*

If something is **small**, it is not large in size or amount.
She is small for her age.

> *Tip:* Some words that rhyme with **small**:
> **all   ball   call   fall   tall**

smell *noun*

The **smell** of something is what you notice about it when you breathe in through your nose.
There was a horrible smell in the fridge.

> *Tip:* Some words that rhyme with **smell**:
> **bell   fell   sell   tell   well**

snail *noun*

A **snail** is a small animal with a long, soft body, no legs, and a round shell on its back.

> *Tip:* Some words that rhyme with **snail**:
> **nail   pail   rail   sail   tail**

snake *noun*

A **snake** is a long, thin animal with no legs, that slides along the ground.
My brother used to have a pet snake called Lenny.

> *Tip:* Some words that rhyme with **snake**:
> **bake   cake   lake   make   take**

snow *noun*

Snow is pieces of soft white frozen water that fall from the sky.
*A lot of **snow** fell last night.*

snowman *noun*

A **snowman** is snow which has been put together to look like a person.
*Last winter we built a huge **snowman**.*

> *Tip:* The word **snowman** is made up of two words: "snow" and "man".

sock *noun*

Socks are pieces of cloth that you wear over your foot and ankle.
*I have a pair of stripy **socks**.*

> *Tip:* Some words that rhyme with **sock**:
> **block   clock   lock   rock**

sofa *noun*

A **sofa** is a long, comfortable seat with a back, that two or three people can sit on.

soup *noun*

Soup is liquid food made by boiling meat, fish, or vegetables in water.

spaghetti *noun*

Spaghetti is long thin pieces of pasta.
*I love **spaghetti** bolognese.*

> *Tip:* The word **spaghetti** comes from Italy.

spider *noun*

A **spider** is a small animal with eight legs.
*Mum, there's a **spider** in the bath!*

spoon *noun*

A **spoon** is a long tool with a round end that is used for eating, serving or mixing food.
*He stirred his coffee with a **spoon**.*

square *noun*

A **square** is a shape with four straight sides that are all the same length.

→ Look at page 78 for more **shapes**.

squirrel *noun*

A **squirrel** is a small animal with a long thick tail. **Squirrels** live in trees.

stairs *noun*

Stairs are steps you walk down or up in a building.
*He walked up the **stairs**.*

a b c d e f g h i j k l m n o p q r **s** t u v w x y z

star *noun*

1 A **star** is a large ball of burning gas in space. **Stars** look like small points of light in the sky.
Stars lit the sky.

2 A **star** is a shape that has four, five, or more points sticking out of it in a pattern.

→ *Look at page 78 for more **shapes**.*

> *Tip:* Some words that rhyme with **star**:
> **bar**   **car**   **far**   **tar**

starfish *noun*

A **starfish** is a flat sea animal. Many **starfish** have five arms.

> *Tip:* The word **starfish** is made up of two words: "star" and "fish".

station *noun*

A **station** is a place where trains or buses stop so that people can get on or off.
*I walked to the bus **station**.*

stick *noun*

A **stick** is a long, thin piece of wood.
*She put some dry **sticks** on the fire.*

> *Tip:* Some words that rhyme with **stick**:
> **kick**   **lick**   **quick**   **tick**   **trick**

sticker *noun*

A **sticker** is a small piece of paper with writing or a picture on it that you stick onto something.
*She gave me a **sticker** for being kind.*

stone *noun*

A **stone** is a small piece of rock that is found on the ground.
*He took a **stone** out of his shoe.*

stop *verb*

If you **stop** doing something, you do not do it any more.
***Stop** throwing those stones!*

> *Tip:* Some words that rhyme with **stop**:
> **hop**   **mop**   **pop**   **shop**   **top**

story *noun*

When someone tells you a **story** they describe people and things that are not real, in a way that makes you enjoy hearing about them.
*This a **story** about four little rabbits.*

strawberry *noun*

A **strawberry** is a small soft red fruit that has a lot of very small seeds on its skin.
*Could I please have some **strawberries** and cream?*

> *Tip:* The word **strawberry** is made up of two words: "straw" and "berry".

strong adjective

Someone who is **strong** is healthy with good muscles.

*He's **strong** enough to carry me.*

sugar noun

Sugar is a sweet thing that is used for making food and drinks taste sweet.

*Do you take **sugar** in your coffee?*

sum noun

In maths, a **sum** is a problem you work out using numbers.

*I have to finish these **sums**.*

sun noun

The **sun** is the large ball of burning gas in the sky that gives us light.

*The **sun** was now high in the sky.*

Tip: Some words that rhyme with **sun**:

| bun | fun | gun | run |

swan noun

A **swan** is a large bird with a long neck, that lives on rivers and lakes.

sweet noun

Sweets are foods that have a lot of sugar.

*Don't eat too many **sweets**.*

swim verb

When you **swim**, you move through water by moving your arms and legs.

*He learned to **swim** when he was three.*

swimming pool noun

A **swimming pool** is a place made for people to swim in.

swing noun

A **swing** is a piece of playground equipment that you sit on and it moves backwards and forwards.

*I love playing on the **swing**.*

sword noun

A **sword** is like a long knife, with a handle and a long sharp blade.

Tip: You do not say the "w" in the word **sword**. It sounds like **board**.

a b c d e f g h i j k l m n o p q r **s** t u v w x y z

Tt

table *noun*

A **table** is a piece of furniture that has legs and a flat top.

tadpole *noun*

A **tadpole** is a small black animal with a round head and a long tail that lives in water. **Tadpoles** grow into frogs or toads.

tail *noun*

An animal's **tail** is the long, thin part at the end of its body.

Tip: Some words that rhyme with **tail**:
nail　**pail**　**rail**　**sail**　**snail**

tap *noun*

A **tap** is a handle which you move to let water run out.
*Make sure you turn the **tap** off!*

tea *noun*

Tea is a drink. You make it by pouring hot water on to the dry leaves of a plant called the **tea** bush.
*I've put the kettle on to make a cup of **tea**.*

teacher *noun*

A **teacher** is a person whose job is to teach other people. **Teachers** usually work in schools.

team *noun*

A **team** is a group of people who work together, or who play a sport together against another group.
*He is in the school football **team**.*

teddy *noun*

A **teddy** is a child's soft toy which looks like a friendly bear.

Tip: The **teddy** was named after a famous American president.

television *noun*

A **television** is a machine that shows moving pictures with sound on a screen.

tennis *noun*

Tennis is a game in which two or four players hit a ball over a net.

tent *noun*

A **tent** is made of strong material that is held up with long pieces of metal and ropes. You sleep in a **tent** when you stay in a camp.

thank _verb_

When you **thank** someone, you tell them that you are pleased about something they have given you or have done for you. You usually do this by saying "Thank you".

thumb _noun_

Your **thumb** is the short, thick finger on the side of your hand.
The baby sucked its **thumb**.

> _Tip:_ You do not say the "b" in the word **thumb**. It sounds like **mum**.

thunder _noun_

Thunder is the loud noise that you sometimes hear from the sky when there is a storm.

tiger _noun_

A **tiger** is a large wild cat that has orange fur with black stripes.

tights _noun_

Tights are a piece of clothing for your legs and feet to keep them warm.

time _noun_

The **time** is a moment in the day that you describe in hours and minutes.
"What **time** is it?" –
"Three o'clock."

toast _noun_

Toast is bread made brown and crisp by heating it.
I had **toast** for breakfast.

toe _noun_

Your **toes** are the five parts at the end of each foot.
I'm sorry I stood on your **toe**.

tomato _noun_

A **tomato** is a soft red fruit with a lot of juice.

tongue _noun_

Your **tongue** is the soft part inside your mouth that moves when you eat or talk.
It's rude to stick your **tongue** out.

tooth _noun_

Your **teeth** are the hard, white things in your mouth that you use to bite and chew food.
I clean my **teeth** twice a day.

toothbrush _noun_

A **toothbrush** is a small brush that you use for cleaning your teeth.
I need a new **toothbrush**.

> _Tip:_ The word **toothbrush** is made up of two words: "tooth" and "brush".

top *noun*

The **top** of something is the highest part of it.
*We climbed to the **top** of the hill.*

> *Tip:* Some words that rhyme with **top**:
> **hop   mop   pop   shop   stop**

tortoise *noun*

A **tortoise** is an animal with a hard shell on its back that moves very slowly. It can pull its head and legs inside the shell. **Tortoises** live on land.

towel *noun*

A **towel** is a piece of thick, soft cloth that you use to get yourself dry.

town *noun*

A **town** is a place with a lot of streets, buildings, and shops, where people live and work.

> *Tip:* Some words that rhyme with **town**:
> **brown clown crown down frown**

toy *noun*

A **toy** is something that you play with.

tractor *noun*

A **tractor** is a vehicle with big wheels at the back. **Tractors** are used on a farm to pull machines and other heavy things.

train *noun*

A **train** is a long vehicle that is pulled by an engine along a railway line.

trainer *noun*

Trainers are shoes that people often wear for running or jogging.
*On Saturday I'm going to get some new **trainers**.*

treasure *noun*

Treasure is valuable things like gold or jewellery.
*The map showed where the **treasure** was hidden.*

tree *noun*

A **tree** is a very tall plant with branches, leaves, and a hard main part that is called a trunk.

Tip: Some words that rhyme with **tree**:
bee   free   knee   see   three

triangle *noun*

A **triangle** is a shape with three straight sides.

→ *Look at page 78 for more* **shapes**.

trousers *noun*

Trousers are things that you can wear. They cover the part of your body below the waist, and each leg.
He was wearing old **trousers**.

truck *noun*

A **truck** is a large vehicle that is used to carry things.
What kind of **truck** *is that?*

Tip: Some words that rhyme with **truck**:
duck   luck   muck   stuck   suck

try *verb*

If you **try** to do something, you do it as well as you can.
I will **try** *to come tomorrow.*

T-shirt *noun*

A **T-shirt** is a short-sleeved shirt with no collar.

tummy *noun*

Your **tummy** is the place inside your body where food goes when you eat it.
I've got a sore **tummy**.

tunnel *noun*

A **tunnel** is a long hole that goes below the ground or through a hill.

TV *noun*

TV is short for "television".
What's on **TV**?

twin *noun*

If two people are **twins**, they have the same parents and they were born on the same day. **Twins** often look alike.

Tip: Some words that rhyme with **twin**:
bin   chin   pin   tin   win

Uu

ugly *adjective*

If something is **ugly**, it is not nice to look at.
*The monster had an **ugly** face.*

umbrella *noun*

An **umbrella** is a long stick that is joined to a cover made of cloth or plastic. It keeps you dry in the rain.

uncle *noun*

Your **uncle** is the brother of your mother or father, or the husband of their brother or sister.

unicorn *noun*

A **unicorn** is a pretend animal that looks like a white horse and has a horn coming out of its head.

Tip: The word **unicorn** means "with one horn".

uniform *noun*

A **uniform** is a special set of clothes that some people wear to show what job they do, or some children wear to show which school they go to.
*I put on my school **uniform**.*

up

When something moves **up**, it moves from a lower place to a higher place.
*She ran **up** the stairs.*

upside down

If something is **upside down**, the part that is usually at the bottom is at the top.
*The picture was **upside down**.*

upstairs

If you go **upstairs** in a building, you go to a higher floor.
*I went **upstairs** to bed.*

Tip: The word **upstairs** is made up of two words: "up" and "stairs".

Vv

Ww

van *noun*

A **van** is a covered vehicle larger than a car but smaller than a lorry.

> *Tip:* Some words that rhyme with **van**:
> fan   man   pan   plan   ran

vase *noun*

A **vase** is a jar for flowers.

vegetable *noun*

Vegetables are plants that you can cook and eat.

vet *noun*

A **vet** is a doctor for animals.

> *Tip:* Some words that rhyme with **vet**:
> bet   get   net   pet   wet

violin *noun*

A **violin** is a musical instrument with four strings that is played with a bow.

volcano *noun*

A **volcano** is a mountain that throws out hot, liquid rock and fire.

walk *verb*

When you **walk**, you move along by putting one foot in front of the other.

wall *noun*

A **wall** is one of the sides of a building or a room.

> *Tip:* Some words that rhyme with **wall**:
> all   ball   call   fall   tall

wand *noun*

A **wand** is a long thin stick that magicians use to do magic.
*He waved his **wand** and a rabbit appeared.*

want *verb*

If you **want** something, you would like to have it.
*I **want** a bike for Christmas.*

wash *verb*

If you **wash** something, you clean it using soap and water.

a b c d e f g h i j k l m n o p q r s t u v w x y z

wasp noun

A **wasp** is an insect with wings and yellow and black stripes across its body. **Wasps** can sting people.

watch noun

A **watch** is a small clock that you wear on your wrist.

water noun

Water is a clear liquid that has no colour, taste or smell. It falls from clouds as rain.

wave noun

Waves on the surface of the sea are the parts that move up and down. *The **waves** broke over the rocks.*

wave verb

If you **wave** your hand, you move it from side to side, usually to say hello or goodbye.

web noun

A **web** is the thin net made by a spider from a string that comes out of its body.

website noun

A **website** is a place on the internet that gives you information.

Tip: The word **website** is made up of two words: "web" and "site".

week noun

A **week** is a period of seven days. *This is the last **week** of the holidays.*

→ *Look at page 79 for more about **days and months**.*

weekend noun

The **weekend** is the days at the end of the week, when you do not go to school or work.

Tip: The word **weekend** is made up of two words: "week" and "end".

→ *Look at page 79 for more about **days and months**.*

well

If you do something **well**, you do it in a good way. *He draws **well**.*

welly noun

Wellies are rubber boots that you wear to keep your feet dry. **Welly** is short for "wellington boot".

Tip: The wellington boot was named after a famous duke.

wet adjective

If something is **wet**, it is covered in water.

Tip: Some words that rhyme with **wet**:
bet   **get**   **net**   **pet**   **vet**

whale *noun*

Whales are very large sea mammals. *Whales breathe through a hole on the top of their heads.*

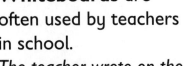

wheel *noun*

Wheels are round and they turn. Bikes and cars move along on **wheels**.

wheelchair *noun*

A **wheelchair** is a chair with wheels that you use if you cannot walk.

Tip: The word **wheelchair** is made up of two words: "wheel" and "chair".

white *noun*

White is the colour of snow or milk. *His shirt is **white**.*

→ *Look at page 78 for more **colours**.*

whiteboard *noun*

A **whiteboard** is a large screen that works with a computer. **Whiteboards** are often used by teachers in school. *The teacher wrote on the **whiteboard**.*

Tip: The word **whiteboard** is made up of two words: "white" and "board".

win *verb*

If you **win**, you do better than everyone. *I've always wanted to **win** first prize!*

Tip: Some words that rhyme with **win**:
| bin | chin | pin | tin | twin |

window *noun*

A **window** is a space in the wall of a building or in the side of a vehicle that has glass in it.

windy *adjective*

If it is **windy**, the wind is blowing hard. *I like flying my kite when it's **windy**.*

wing *noun*

The **wings** of birds, insects or aeroplanes are the parts that keep them in the air.

Tip: Some words that rhyme with **wing**:
| king | ring | sing | thing |

witch *noun*

In children's stories, a **witch** is a woman who has magic powers that she sometimes uses to do bad things.

wizard *noun*

In children's stories, a **wizard** is a man who has magic powers.

a b c d e f g h i j k l m n o p q r s t u v w x y z

wolf *noun*

A **wolf** is a wild animal that looks like a large dog.

wood *noun*

1 **Wood** is the hard material that trees are made of.
The table and chairs were made of ***wood***.

2 A **wood** is a large area of trees growing near each other.
The children didn't want to get lost in the ***wood***.

world *noun*

The **world** is the earth, the planet we live on.

worm *noun*

A **worm** is a small animal with a long thin body, no bones, and no legs.

write *verb*

When you **write** something, you use a pen or pencil to make letters, words, or numbers.
She told her to ***write*** *her name in full.*

> *Tip:* You do not say the "w" in the word **write**. It sounds like **bite**.

Xx

X-ray *noun*

An **X-ray** is a picture of the inside of someone's body.
The ***X-ray*** *showed that my foot was broken.*

xylophone *noun*

A **xylophone** is an instrument made of flat pieces of wood in a row. You hit the pieces with a stick to make different sounds.

> *Tip:* The word **xylophone** comes from Greece.

Yy

year *noun*

A **year** is a period of twelve months.

> *Tip:* Some words that rhyme with **year**:
> ear   fear   gear   hear   near

➡ *Look at page 79 for more about* ***days and months***.

yellow *noun*

Yellow is the colour of lemons or butter.
Her favourite colour is ***yellow***.

➡ *Look at page 78 for more* ***colours***.

yes

You say **yes** to agree with someone or something, or if you want something.

yogurt, yoghurt *noun*

Yogurt is a thick liquid food that is made from milk.

yo-yo *noun*

A **yo-yo** is a toy that is fastened to a piece of string. You play by making the **yo-yo** go up and down on the string.

Zz

zebra *noun*

A **zebra** is a wild African animal like a horse with black and white stripes.

zebra crossing *noun*

A **zebra crossing** is a place where you can cross the road safely. It is shown by black and white stripes on the road.

zip *noun*

A **zip** is two long rows of little teeth and a piece that slides along them. You pull this to open or close the **zip**.

> *Tip:* Some words that rhyme with **zip**:
> chip   lip   nip   ship   skip

zoo *noun*

A **zoo** is a place where animals are kept so that people can look at them.

a b c d e f g h i j k l m n o p q r s t u v w x y z

Colours and shapes

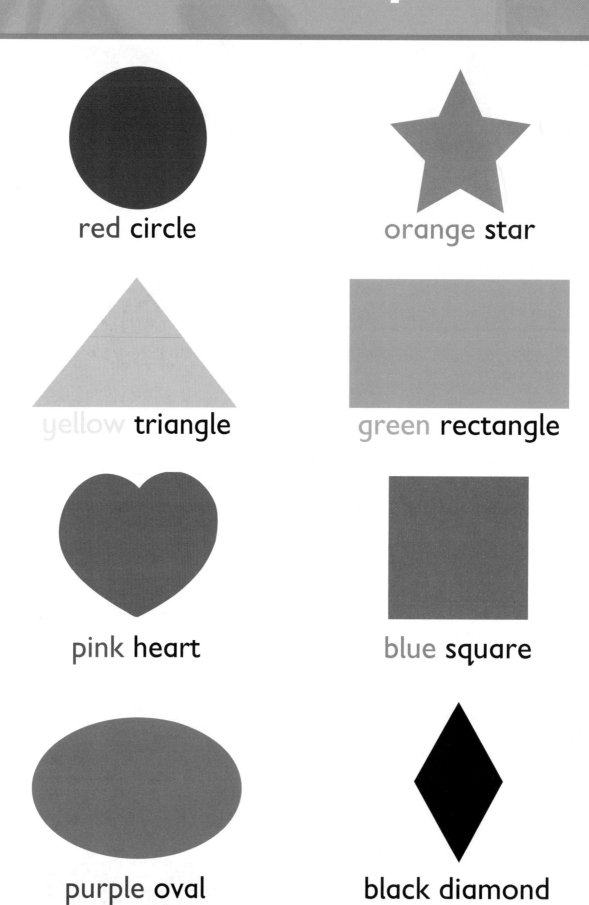

red circle

orange star

yellow triangle

green rectangle

pink heart

blue square

purple oval

black diamond

Days and months

Monday

Tuesday

Wednesday

Thursday

Friday

Saturday

Sunday

★ ★

January

February

March

April

May

June

July

August

September

October

November

December

Numbers

1 one	21 twenty-one
2 two	22 twenty-two
3 three	23 twenty-three
4 four	24 twenty-four
5 five	25 twenty-five
6 six	26 twenty-six
7 seven	27 twenty-seven
8 eight	28 twenty-eight
9 nine	29 twenty-nine
10 ten	30 thirty
11 eleven	40 forty
12 twelve	50 fifty
13 thirteen	60 sixty
14 fourteen	70 seventy
15 fifteen	80 eighty
16 sixteen	90 ninety
17 seventeen	100 hundred
18 eighteen	101 a hundred and one
19 nineteen	1 000 a thousand
20 twenty	1 000 000 a million